Dedicated to Savy and Peanut, who make every day an adventure. Thank you for traveling the world with us.

NATIVE AMERICA

Educational Resources, Crafts & Activities for Kids

Sarah M. Prowant, MSN-Ed, RN

Savy Activities
Colorado, USA

TERMS & CONDITIONS

FOR BEST RESULTS:

When assembling a 3D model, glue a second piece of thick paper with a craft glue stick to back of each sheet of model pieces (prior to cutting pieces) to provide additional stability when assembled.

Laminate all cards & posters with at least 3 ml lamination for additional protection.

If printing from an ebook, cardstock paper (>60 lbs) provides best results for cards, models and manipulative activities, while standard printer paper is adequate for recipes, lessons, etc. Please set printer to "FIT TO PAGE" when printing for best results.

FOLLOW US ON SOCIAL MEDIA!

@savyactivities

/SavyActivities

www.SavyActivities.com

WHATS INCLUDED:

- North American Continent/Territories Tribe Pinning
- Native American Facts
- Native American History Timeline Poster
- Native American Alphabet Cards
- Native American Landmark Pinning
- Turtle Island Mini-Book
- Petroglyph/graph Art
- Cherokee Syllabary Poster
- Native American Dwellings Info Cards
- Wigwam, Longhouse, Tipi, Adobe, Grass House, Chickee, Igloo & Plank House Model
- Native American Sensory Bin
- North American Fauna 3-Part Cards
- North American Animal Tracks
- Life Cycle, Parts of & Tracing Bison
- Bison vs. Buffalo Venn Diagram & Mask
- Buffalo Felt Puzzle Craft
- Bow & Arrow Craft
- Finish the Pattern: Arrowheads
- Potato Arrowhead Carving
- Three Sisters Poster
- Corn Kernel Removal
- Beaded Rainbow Corn
- Corn Husk Doll
- Paper Roll Totem
- Gourd Drums
- Dream Catcher
- Native American Warrior Poster
- Moccasin Lacing
- Fry Bread Recipe
- Historic Native Americans (Info Cards)
- Native American Canoe
- Grasslands Habitat Match
- North American Bird Feather Matching
- Southern Native Designs Matching

North America Continent

Native American Territories

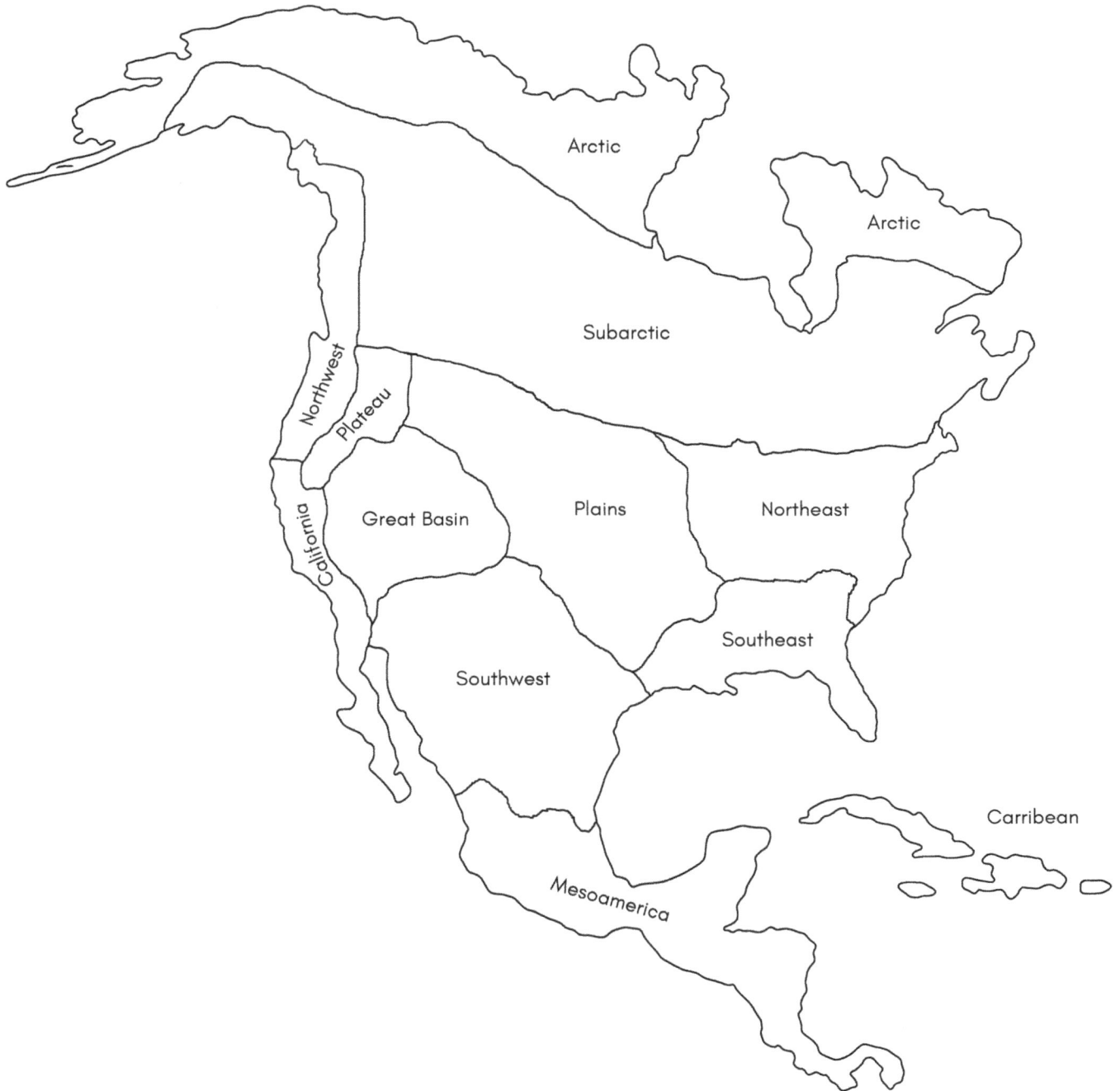

Arctic

Arctic

Subarctic

Northwest

Plateau

California

Great Basin

Plains

Northeast

Southwest

Southeast

Carribean

Mesoamerica

Native American Tribes

List is not comprehensive; represents a few of the more commonly known tribes. Labels can be used to identify geographical locations on map or as a list to study independently.

Chinook	Nez Perce	Navajo
Yakima	Pomo	Apache
Paiute	Shoshone	Pueblo
Ute	Pawnee	Crow
Cheyenne	Arapaho	Comanche
Natchez	Choctaw	Chickasaw
Seminole	Creek	Cherokee
Powhatan	Miami	Shawnee
Iroquois	Sioux	Pequot
Massachuset	Abenaki	Inuit
Mohawk	Tlingit	Aleut

Native American Facts

The word "barbecue" is from the Arawakan Indian language meaning "framework of sticks."

The Iroquois began the tradition of trick-or-treating. Iroquois children would be led around the village, collecting gifts.

Most indigenous people refer to themselves as "American Indian", "First Nations", or "Native Americans".

The Nez Perce people helped Lewis and Clark explore the Northwest Territory by building canoes, drawing maps and guiding.

Northwest Native Americans built totem poles of special animals or as a memorial to their ancestors.

The Sequoia tree is named in honor of the Cherokee leader Sequoyah, who helped his people develop an alphabet.

Native Americans invented the modern game of hockey, which originated from their game of "shinny".

The term "Indian" originated with Christopher Columbus who thought he had landed in the East Indies.

Native American Facts

Native Americans created a red dye out of dried insects, called cochineal.

Native Americans were the first to use anesthetics. Previously, European doctors performed surgery without any drugs.

More than half of US states have names based on Native languages, like Connecticut, Utah, and Kentucky.

The Navajo Nation has the largest tribal land in the United States.

There are 574 federally recognized Native American tribes.

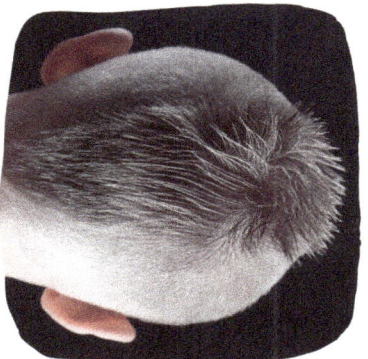

The Iroquois called maize, beans, and squash the "three sisters."

The Mohawk hairstyle is named after the Mohawks, one of the tribes that made up the Iroquois nation.

Lacrosse was first played by people of the Southeast, especially the Choctaw.

Timeline of Native American History

13,000 BC — First people come to America

AD

1492 — Columbus calls Native Americans "Indians"

1595 — Pocahontas is born

1621 — The First Thanksgiving

1763 — Battle of Bloody Run

1785 — Treaty of Hopewell

1803 — Sacagawea guides Lewis and Clark

1809 — Sequoyah creates Native American alphabet

1831 — Indian Removal Act begins Trail of Tears

1868 — Battle of Little Bighorn (Custer's Last Stand)

1879 — Carlisle Indian School opens

1890 — Wounded Knee Massacre

1912 — Jim "Wa-Tho-Huk" Thorpe wins at Olympic games

1924 — Indian Citizenship Act is passed

1929 — Charles Curtis becomes US Vice President

1968 — Indian Civil Rights Act is passed

1975 — Indian Self Determination & Education Act

2020 — NFL team "Redskins" changes name to "Commanders"

2021 — MLB team "Indians" changes name to "Guardians"

Native American Alphabet

Aa

Bb

Cc

Dd

Ee

Ff

Gg

Hh

Ii

Jj

Kk

Ll

Mm

Nn

Oo

Pp

Qq

Rr

Ss

Tt

Vv

Uu

Ww

Xx

Yy

Zz

Native American Alphabet Cards

Aa  Acorn	**Ee**  Eagle
Bb 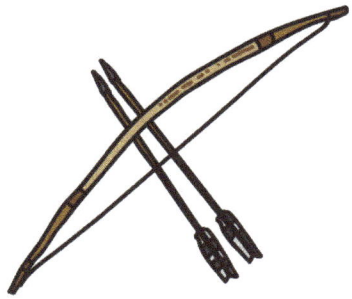 Bow & Arrow	**Ff**  Flute
Cc 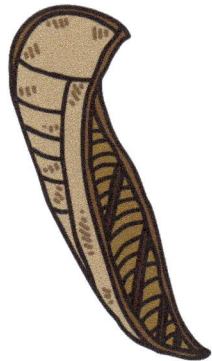 Canoe	**Gg**  Great Spirit
Dd 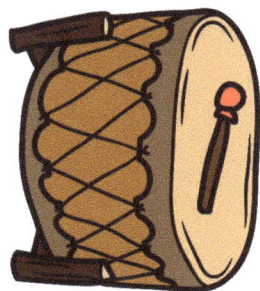 Drum	**Hh**  Headdress

Native American Alphabet Cards

Ii

Inuit

Mm

Maize

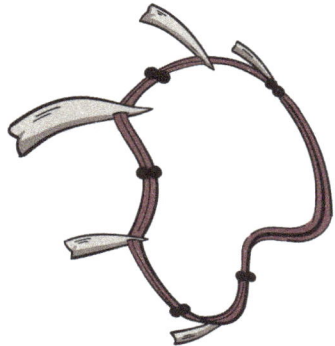

Jj

Jewelry

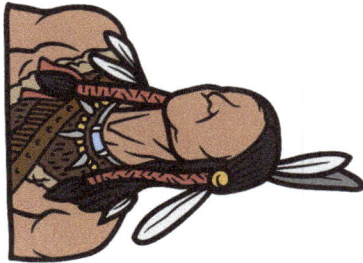

Nn

Navajo

Kk

Knife

Oo

Owl

Ll

Lizard

Pp

Papoose

Native American Alphabet Cards

Qq Qajaq	**Uu** Ute
Rr Rattle	**Vv** Violet
Ss Smoke Signal	**Ww** Warrior
Tt Tomahawk	**Xx** Xat

Native American Alphabet Cards

Zinnia

Zz

Yucca

Yy

Native American Landmarks

Cut out circles using a 1" circle punch or scissors. Place circles on map where the landmarks are located. Refer to the control version for help if needed.

Mesa Verde, CO

Casa Grande, AZ

Effigy Mounds, IA

**Organ Mountains-
Desert Peaks, NM**

**Chaco
Culture, NM**

**Hopewell
Culture, OH**

Aztec Ruins, NM

**Gila Cliff
Dwellings, NM**

Wupatki, AZ

Devils Tower, WY

**Montezuma
Castle, AZ**

Hovenweep, AZ

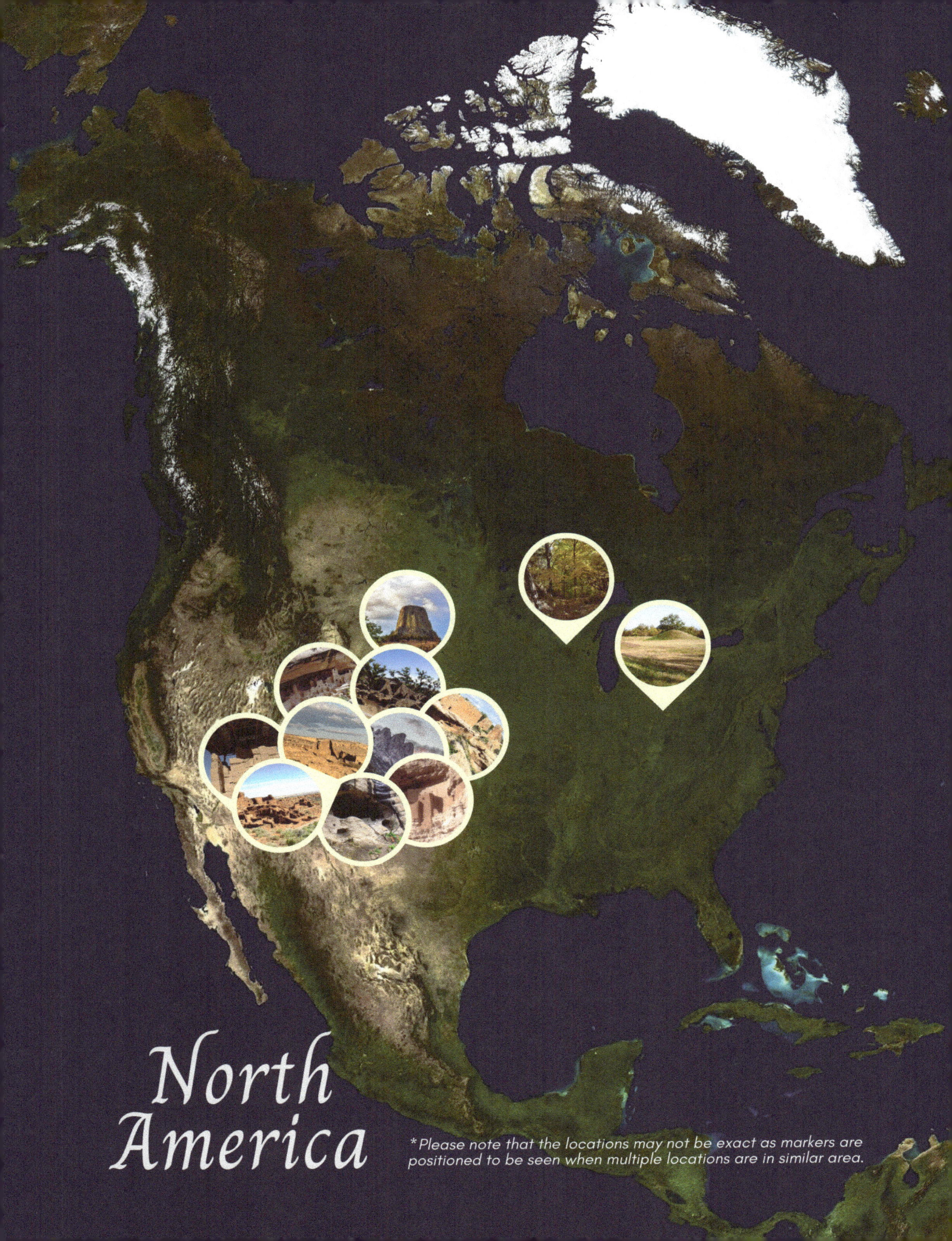

North America

*Please note that the locations may not be exact as markers are positioned to be seen when multiple locations are in similar area.

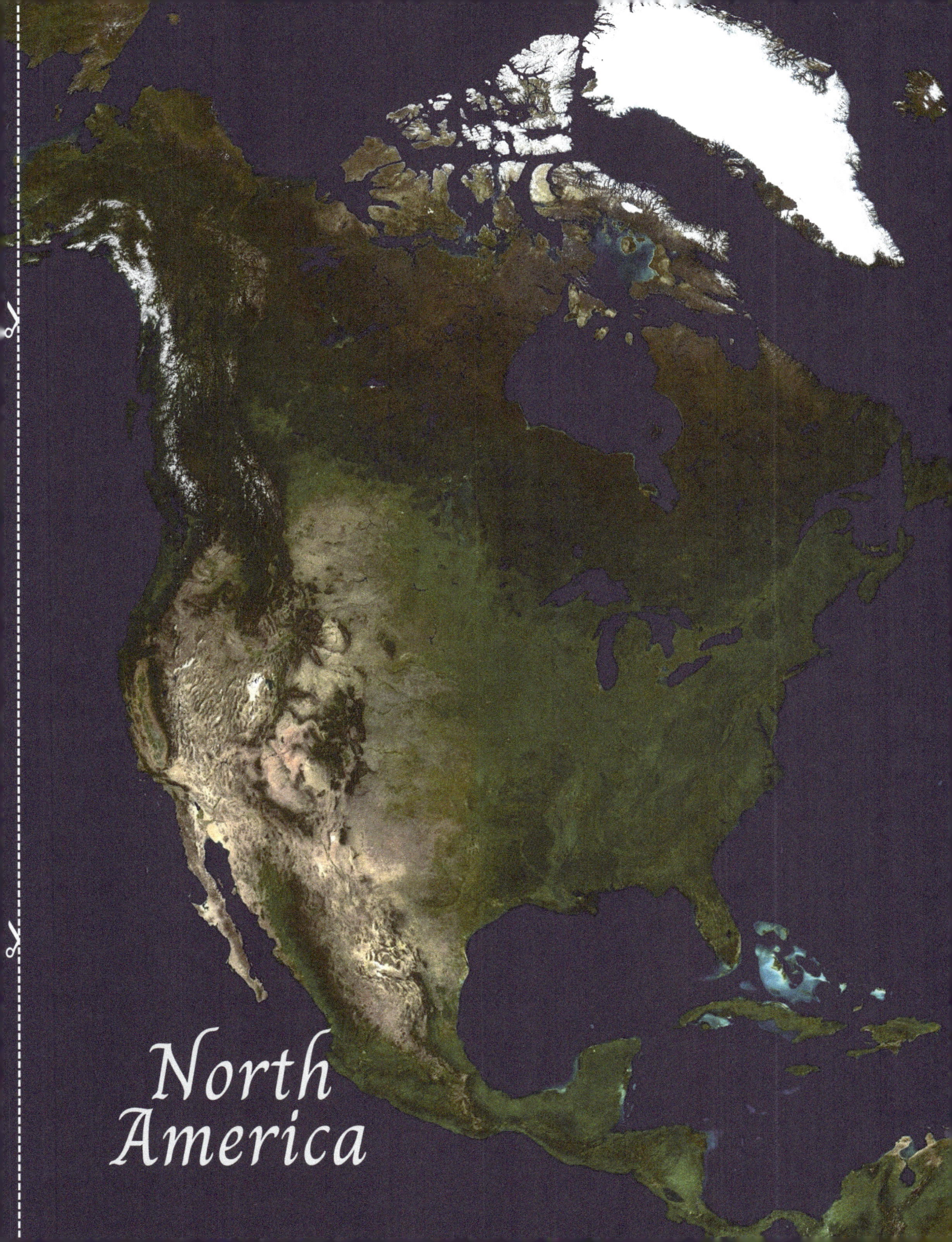

North America

TURTLE ISLAND

The turtle said that if the muskrat was willing to give his life, he could give them his shell. They put the earth that the Muskrat had brought back onto his shell. The earth began to grow, which also caused the turtle to grow.

9

One day, the people stopped getting along and started fighting. It became so bad that the Great Spirit decided to wash it all away with lots of water.

2

Once upon a time, before the earth was created, people lived on a great island floating in space. It was a wonderful place, and everyone lived together without any problems.

1

The turtle continued to grow bigger and bigger and the dirt continued to multiply until it became a huge expanse of land, which they now refer to as Turtle Island.

THE END.

10

A great flood came, and the beautiful place fell to the earth and was covered in water. Only the animals and Nanabush, the sky man, survived.

3

Finally the muskrat offered to try; he took a deep breath and dove down. The other animals and Nanabush waited. Lots of time passed, but the muskrat didn't appear. Finally they saw him! Everyone swam to him. The dive proved too much for the muskrat, and as he breathed his last breath, the animals and Nanabush noticed that he was clutching earth he had brought up from the depths.

8

The turtle tried, but he was used to walking on land, not swimming in the sea.

7

Everyone was sad because they no longer had a dry place to live. As they floated in the water, Nanabush, had a great idea.

4

Assembly Instructions

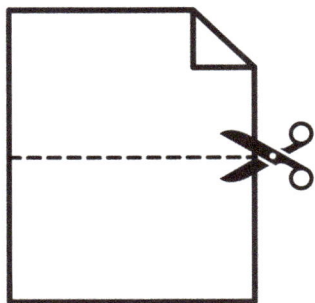

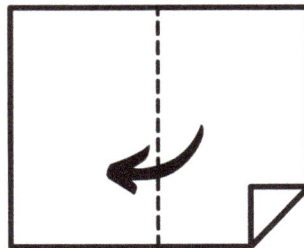

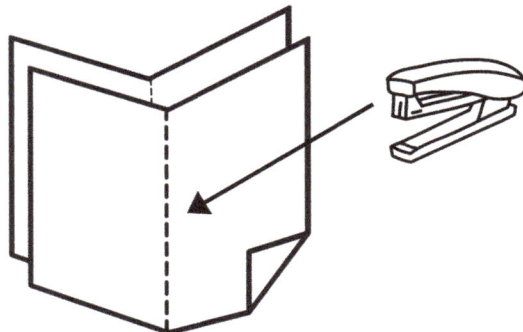

Cut paper in half on lines. Fold each page of book as indicated. Collate together so pages match up appropriately. Staple spine to hold together.

Nanabush decided to swim to the bottom of the ocean and bring back some earth to create some new land. But no matter how hard he tried, he couldn't reach the bottom.

5

The animals all tried to retrieve soil to recreate the earth, but one by one they all failed.

The loon tried, but he was used to flying in the sky, not swimming below the water.

6

PETROGLYPH/ PICTOGRAPH ART

Instructions

Petroglyphs are carved images, incised or scratched into stone. A pictograph is a painting on stone, using natural pigments. Both pictographs and petroglyphs can be found all over North American, and were ways of communicating and leaving messages with images instead of words. Native American petroglyphs and pictographs include thousands of images and symbols, each with individual meanings. Sometimes, multiple tribes used similar images, but exact meanings could vary. Some symbols stood for human qualities, like wisdom, or ideas like swiftness.

Provide the child with a piece of craft paper (to mimic animal hide) or a large rock. Have them copy some of the symbols on the included template. Compare the pictures to their meanings - what does their story say?

Materials

- Symbols Template
- Kraft Paper
- Rock (optional)
- Markers / Paint

Native American Symbols

Hunt	Peace	Friendship	War	Horse
Horse	Eagle	Deer	Fish	Many Fish
Turtle	Bear	Sun	Moon	Star
Days/Nights	Mountains	River	Rain	Snow
Campfire	Tipi	Hogan	Camp	We
Man	Woman	Happy	Sad	Wise

SEQUOYAH'S
Cherokee Syllabary

D a	R e	T i	Ꮞ o	O u	i v
S ga Ꭳ ka	Ꮅ ge	Ꮵ gi	A go	J gu	E gv
Ꮤ ha	Ꮲ he	Ꮒ hi	Ꮀ ho	Ꮣ hu	Ꮛ hv
W la	Ꮆ le	Ꮑ li	Ꮵ lo	M lu	Ꮜ lv
Ꮉ ma	Ꮻ me	H mi	Ꮭ mo	Ꮗ mu	
Ꮎ na Ꮏ hna Ꮐ nah	Ʌ ne	Ꮒ ni	Ꮓ no	Ꮕ nu	Ꮔ nv
Ꮖ gua	Ꮙ que	Ꮗ qui	Ꮴ quo	Ꮜ quu	Ꮿ quv
Ꮪ sa Ꮝ s	4 se	Ꮥ si	Ꮡ so	Ꮢ su	Ꮧ sv
Ꮣ da Ꮤ ta	Ꮷ de Ꮦ te	Ꮧ di Ꭲ ti	Ꮩ do	Ꮪ du	Ꮫ dv
Ꮬ dla Ꮭ tla	Ꮮ tle	Ꮯ tli	Ꮰ tlo	Ꮱ tlu	Ꮲ tlv
Ꮳ tsa	Ꮴ tse	Ꮵ tsi	Ꮶ tso	Ꮷ tsu	Ꮸ tsv
Ꮹ wa	Ꮻ we	Ꮼ wi	Ꮼ wo	Ꮽ wu	Ꮾ wv
Ꮿ ya	Ᏼ ye	Ꭵ yi	Ꭹ yo	Ꭼ yu	Ᏼ yv

Sounds Represented by Vowels

a, as a in father, or short as a in rival

e, as a in hate, or short as e in met

i, as i in pique, or short as i in pit

o, as o in note, approaching aw in law

u, as oo in fool, or short as u in pull

v, as u in but, nasalized

Consonant Sounds

g nearly as in English, but approaching to k. d nearly as in English, but approaching to t. h k l m n q s t w y as in English. Syllables beginning with g except S (ga) have sometimes the power of k. A (go), S (du), Ꮫ (dv) are sometimes sounded to, tu, tv and syllables written with tl except Ꮭ (tla) sometimes vary to dl.

Native American Dwellings

WIGWAM
Apache, Paiute, Ojibwe, Chiricahua, Ute, Goshute, Wampanoag, etc.

Materials Used

Wigwams were easy to construct from wood, saplings or brush with overlapping mats of a variety of materials, including bark, leather and grasses. This style was used by many different tribes due to its versatile design, with the materials used based on what was available in the area. They were smaller structures, measuring 8-10 feet tall.

LONGHOUSE
Haudenosaunee, Wyandot, Lenni, Lenape, Powhatan, Tsimshian, Makah, Haida, Clatsop, Multonomah, etc.

Materials Used

Longhouses provided shelter for entire clans, as well as community gatherings. Measuring up to 200 feet long, these structures used raised platforms to create a second story, used for sleeping. Mats and wood screens divided the longhouse into separate rooms. At each end were doors, and smoke holes were made between the bark covering.

Native American Dwellings

TIPI

Blackfoot, Arapaho, Assiniboine, Cheyenne, Comanche, Crow, Gros Ventre, Kiowa, Lakota, Lipan, Apache, etc.

Materials Used

Often incorrectly attributed to all Native Americans, the tipi was primarily used by tribes in the Great Plains region. Tipis were usually made of wood and buffalo skins, and often decorated. They had an open area at the top to allow smoke to escape. These homes were easy to move when the tribe relocated.

ADOBE

Pueblo & Hopi

Materials Used

Adobe homes are multi-story houses made of adobe (clay and straw baked into hard bricks) or of large stones cemented together with adobe. Each adobe unit was home to one family, and the entire structure housed the extended clan. Adobe style homes are still used today, and many historic communities have been made into national parks.

Native American Dwellings

GRASS HOUSE
Caddo & Wichita

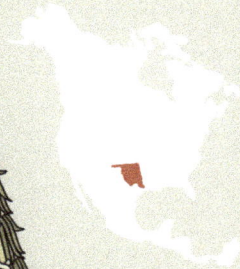

Materials Used

Grass houses were large beehive-shaped structures that served as permanent dwellings in the southern plains nations.

They were built using a framework of long wooden poles bent into a cone shape and thatched with long prairie grass. Some exceeded 40 feet tall!

CHICKEE
Seminoles and Miccosukees

Materials Used

Chickees were open-air structures composed of thatch roofs over a wood frame. The higher floors protected the occupants from flood and wet conditions. The first homes of the area were primarily log cabins, but chickees soon became an effective solution to allow for fast movement away from U.S. troops.

Native American Dwellings

IGLOO
Inuit

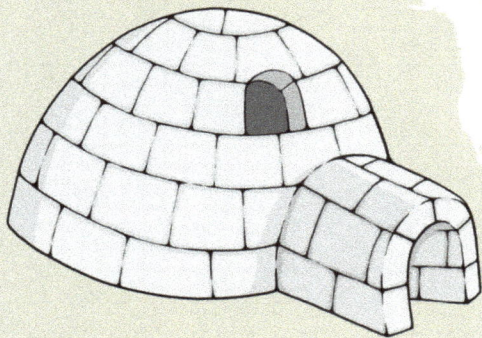

Materials Used

Igloos are created by compacted snow which created a layer of insulation from harsh weather. Igloos usually included a living area, tunnel and ventilation hole. Igloos were frequently used for temporary protection, and other styles of shelters provided permanent living structures.

PLANK HOUSE
Tlingit, Nisga'a, Haida, Heiltsuk, Kwakiutl, Makah, Quileute, Chinookan, Yurok, etc.

Materials Used

Plank houses were created from long, flat planks of wood built over a wooden frame. Some plank houses functioned as longhouses, providing communal spaces for multiple families. Although these structures are similar to old European houses, this style of housing was used on the northwest coast long before Europeans arrived.

WIGWAM MODEL

Instructions

Wigwams (also known as wickiup, wetu) are a versatile design created by building a framework of wood saplings and overlapping mats of a variety of materials, including woven grass, animal skins and bark. This style was used by many different tribes, with variations based on the available supplies in the area.

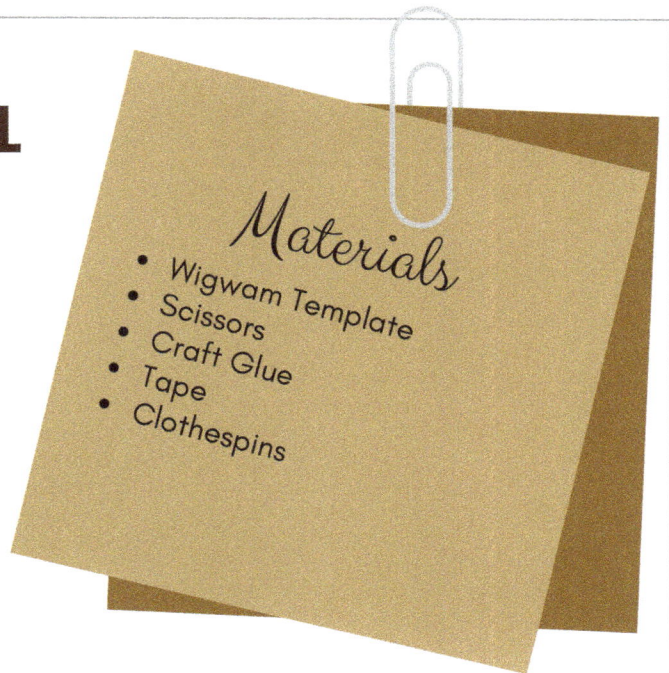

Cut out included wigwam template. Carefully cut out each tab in between each section. Fold the tabs slightly so they can accommodate the curvature of the structure. Starting at the center, glue each tab under the adjacent section to form a domed surface. Secure with craft glue, or for faster construction use tape. If using craft glue, hold pieces in place with clothespins as they dry.

Discuss: What materials near your home would be suitable for a wigwam?

Wigwam

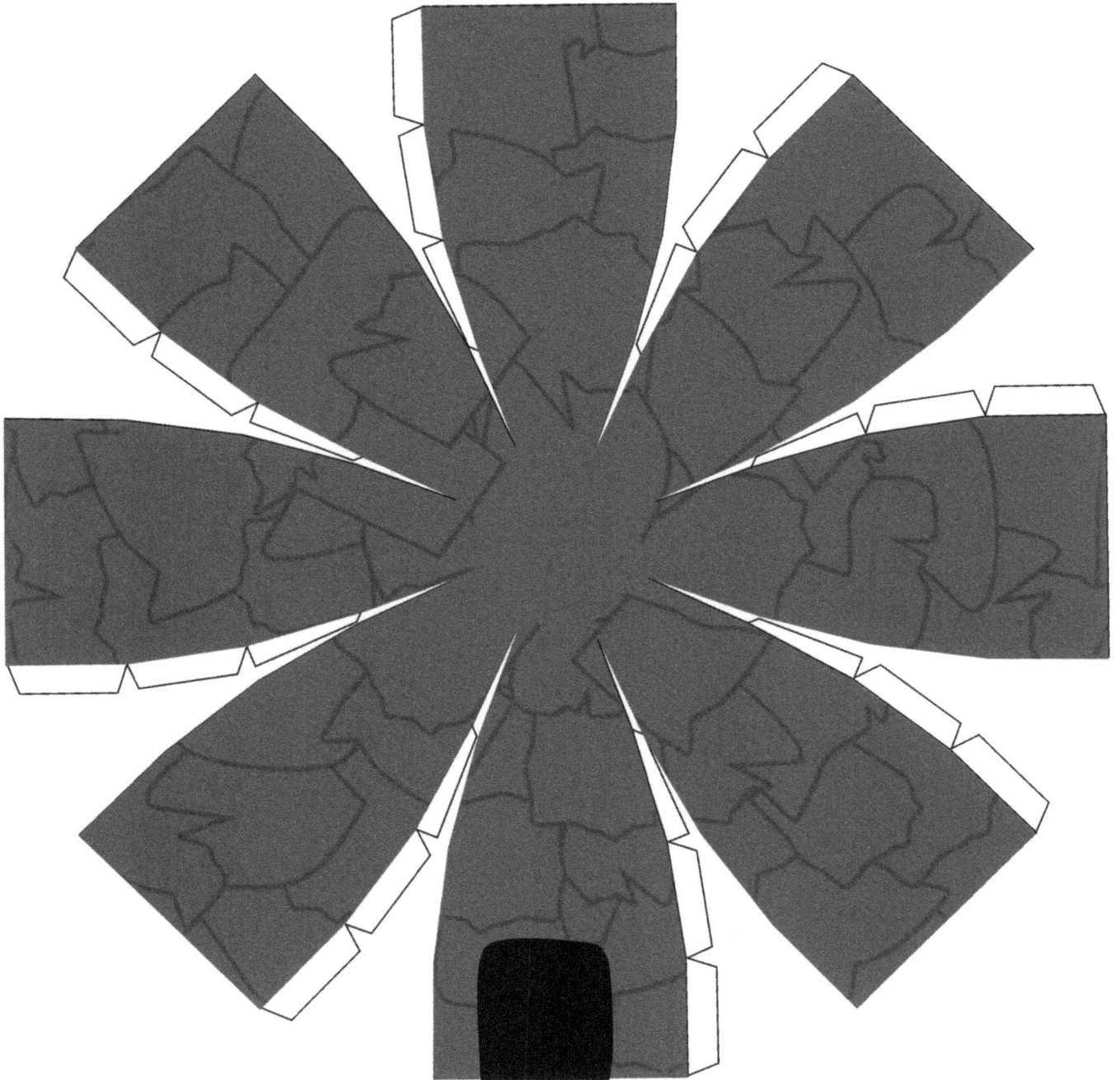

LONGHOUSE MODEL

Instructions

A longhouse or long house is a type of long, proportionately narrow, single-room building. Many were built from timber and often represent the earliest form of permanent structure in many cultures. In Native America, these structures housed multiple families and had second story levels that provided sleeping areas.

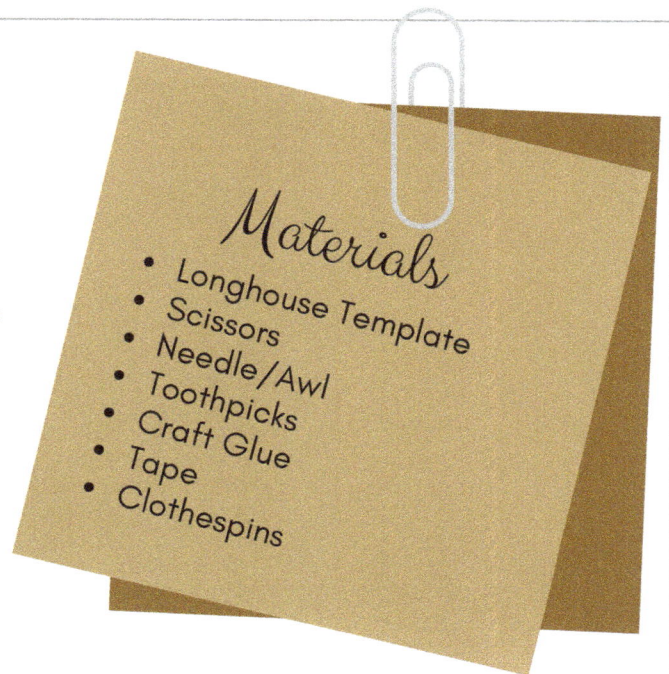

Materials

- Longhouse Template
- Scissors
- Needle/Awl
- Toothpicks
- Craft Glue
- Tape
- Clothespins

Cut out included longhouse template. Fold the tabs on the side inward. Secure to front and back piece with craft glue or tape. Use clothespins to hold pieces together while drying. Allow each section to dry completely before moving on to next section. Roll the roof section to create curvature. Secure to tabs on top of the front and back pieces and sides with craft glue or tape. Cut open the entrance as indicated. Fold upwards to create a entrance covering. Poke small holes in the corners with a large needle or awl. Insert two toothpicks and secure with craft glue. Allow to completely dry. Display!

Longhouse

Longhouse

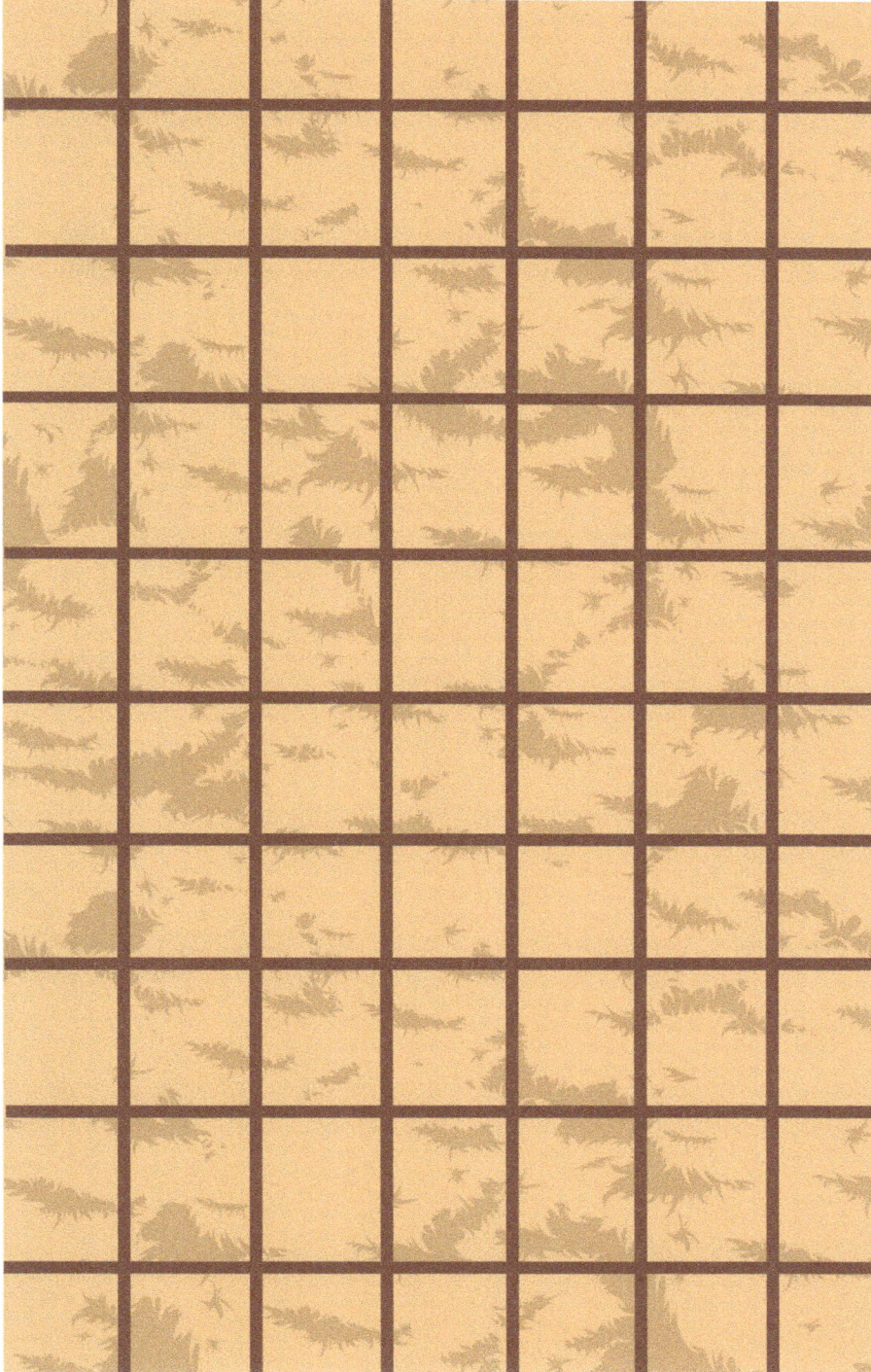

TIPI MODEL

Instructions

A tipi is a tent, traditionally made of animal skins upon wooden poles. Modern tipis usually have a canvas covering. A tipi is distinguished from other tents by the smoke flaps at the top of the structure. Often incorrectly attributed to all Native Americans, this structure was primarily used by the Great Plains tribes.

Materials

- Tipi Template
- Scissors
- Craft Knife
- Craft Glue
- Tape
- Skewer Sticks
- Clothespins

Cut out included tipi template. Use a craft knife to cut out entrance hole - *this step should be completed by an adult or with close adult supervision to avoid injury*. Fold along indicated lines to create a pentagon shape. Fold smoke flaps along indicated lines. Using craft glue, secure skewer sticks along fold lines on the side of the tipi. Allow each skewer stick to dry completely before moving onto the next step. It may be helpful to use a clothespin to keep sticks in place, as they have a tendency to roll around. Glue back of tipi together as indicated. Once the entire structure has dried completely, trim the sticks at the top.

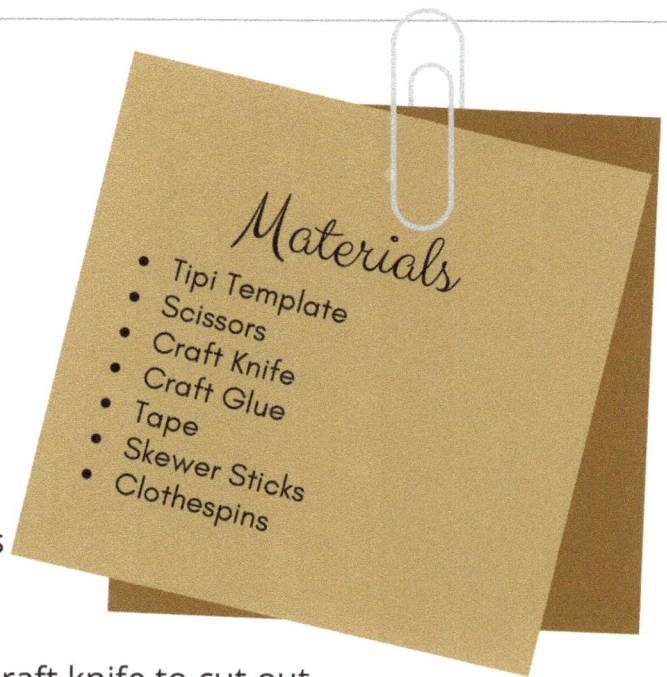

Discuss: What types of Native American structures were you familiar with prior to this activity? Why are tipis recognized more than other Native American structures? What other examples of incorrect assumptions for Native American culture can you think of?

Tipi

Glue Here

Cut Out

ADOBE MODEL

Instructions

Adobe is a building material made from clay, straw, wood & rock. Native Americans often made these as stand-alone buildings or built into the side of cliffs or rocks. These structures were divided into living areas for each family and housing entire clans throughout the complete complex.

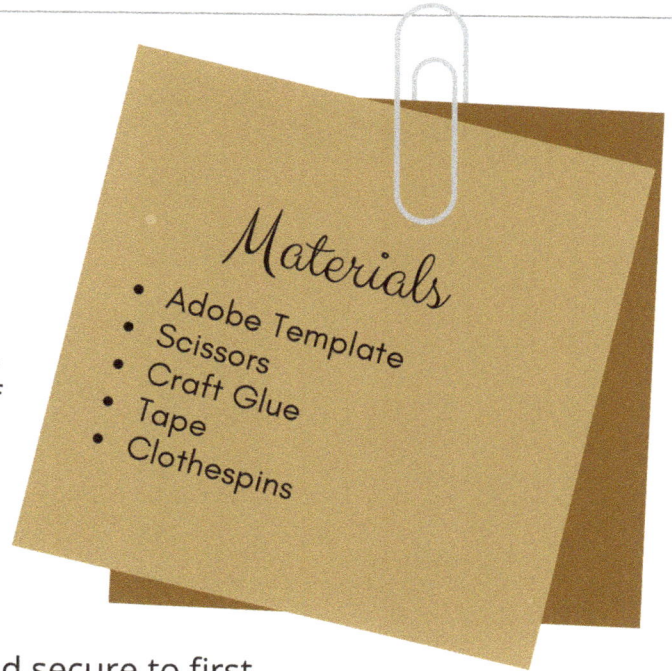

Materials

- Adobe Template
- Scissors
- Craft Glue
- Tape
- Clothespins

Cut out included adobe template.
Assemble included first floor pieces and secure to first floor roof with craft glue or tape. Secure sides of first floor as well. Make sure to allow glue to dry completely before proceeding to next step, if used. It may be helpful to use clothespins to secure pieces during drying process. Locate the second floor roof and secure the second floor pieces to roof. Secure to top of first floor with paint or tape.

Locate the oven template. Fold the tabs slightly to allow for the curvature of the design. Secure the tabs under the adjacent piece to create a three sided cone structure. Glue to first floor roof near the second story.

Discuss: How many people live in your house? How many live in your neighborhood? How close are the houses? Would you like to live near all your extended family?

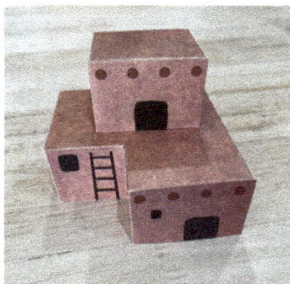

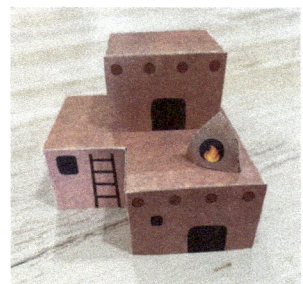

Adobe

Main Floor Roof

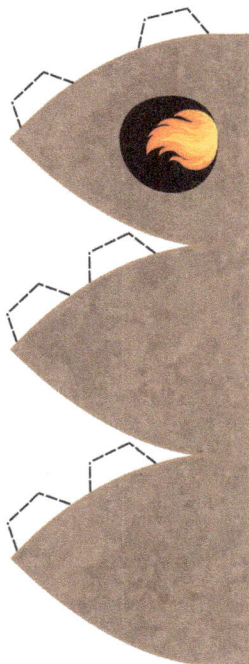

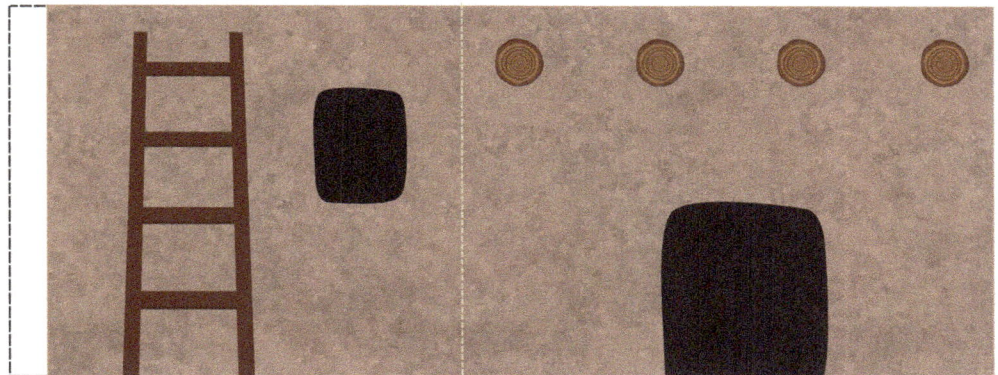

Second Floor Sides

Main Floor Side

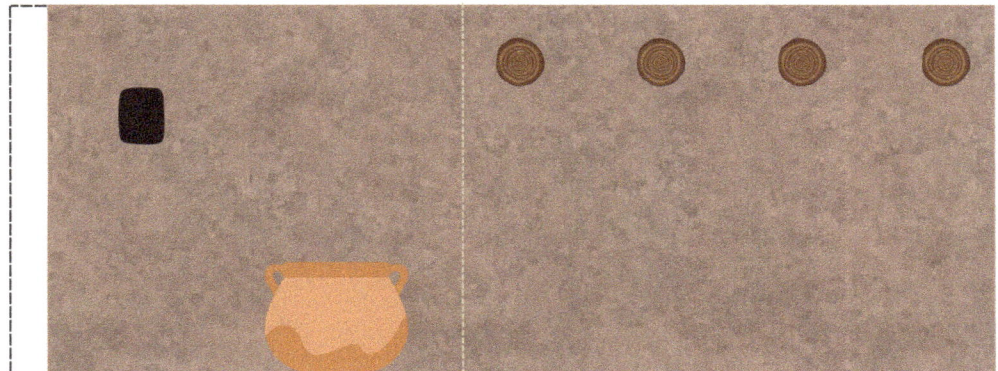

Oven

Adobe

Main Floor Side

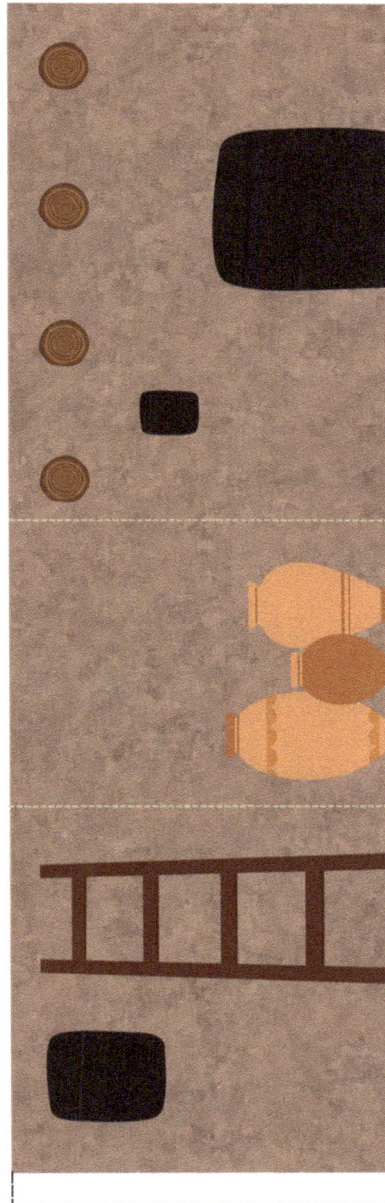

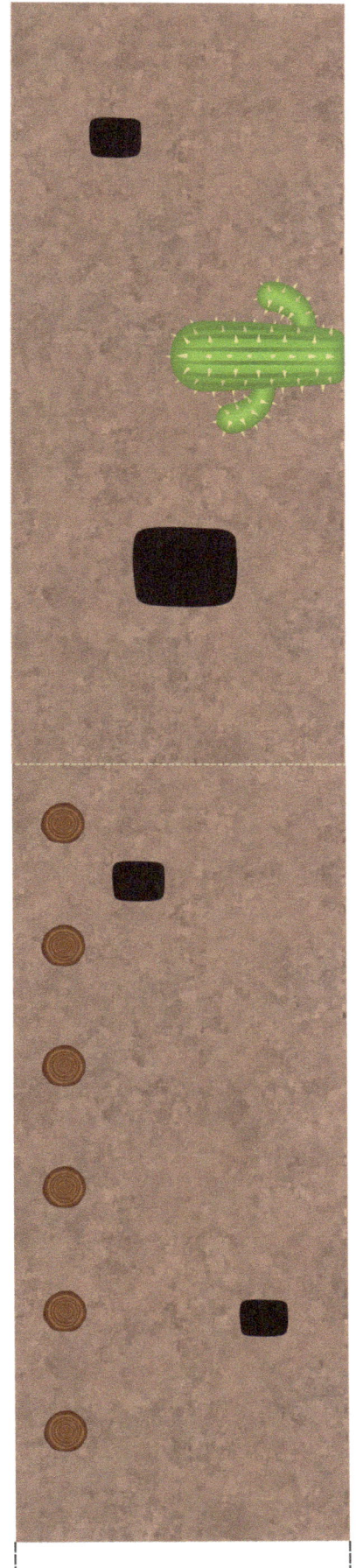

Main Floor Side

Main Floor Side

Second Floor Roof

GRASS HOUSE MODEL

Instructions

Grass houses are American Indian homes used in the Southern Plains region. They resemble large wigwams in many ways. Grass houses are made with a wooden frame bent into a beehive shape and thatched with long prairie grass. These were large buildings, sometimes more than 40 feet tall.

Materials

- Grass House Template
- Scissors
- Craft Glue
- Tape
- Clothespins

Cut out included grass house template. Secure two pieces together as indicated with craft glue or tape. It may be helpful to use clothespins to secure pieces during drying process. Fold the tabs slightly so they can accommodate the curvature of the structure. Starting at the center, glue each tab under the adjacent section to form a cone-shaped surface. Secure with craft glue, or for faster construction, use tape. If using craft glue, hold pieces in place with clothespins as they dry. **Discuss:** What kinds of cone or dome-shaped structures have you seen?

Grass House

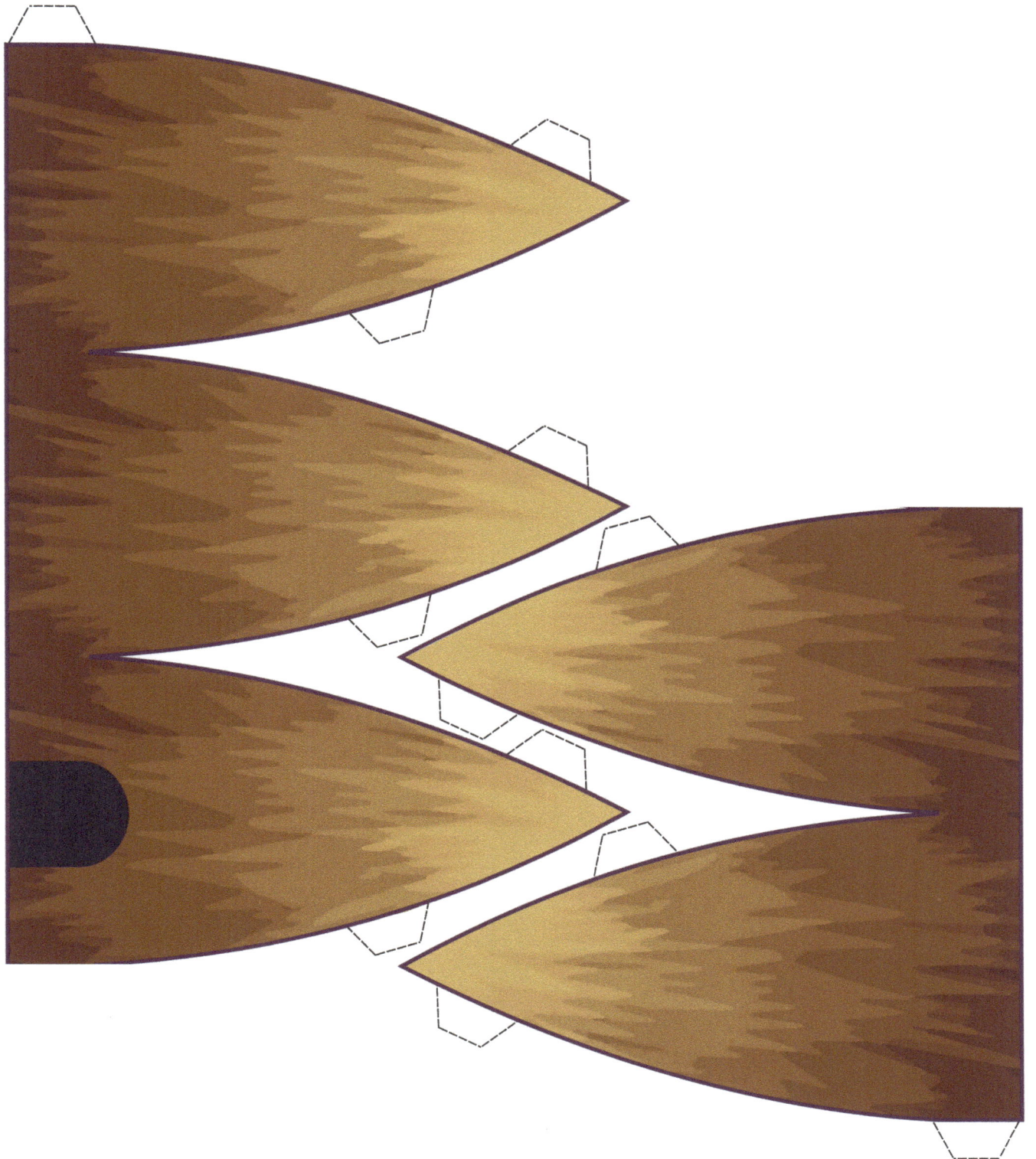

CHICKEE MODEL

Instructions

Chickees (also known as chickee huts, stilt houses or platform dwellings) were used primarily in Florida by tribes like the Seminole Indians. Chickee houses consisted of thick posts supporting a thatched roof and a flat wooden platform raised several feet off the ground, and did not have any walls. During rainstorms, tarps made of hide or cloth would be attach to the chickee frame to keep the occupants dry.

Materials

- Chickee Template
- Scissors
- Craft Knife
- Craft Glue
- Tape
- Clothespins

Cut out included chickee template. Use a craft knife to remove sections between the structures, as indicated - *this step should be completed by an adult or with close adult supervision to avoid injury*. Fold the tabs on the sides and top of the exterior and glue (or tape) together at corners to create a four-sided structure. It may be helpful to use clothespins to secure connections during drying process, if glue is used. Allow to dry completely prior to proceeding to next step. Place floor piece into the center of the structure and secure to sides using glue or tape. Fold the thatched roof down the center as indicated. Connect the roof to the structure along the tabs on the front and back pieces. Allow to dry completely.

Discuss: What kinds of open-air shelters have you seen before? Where were they located? What were they used for?

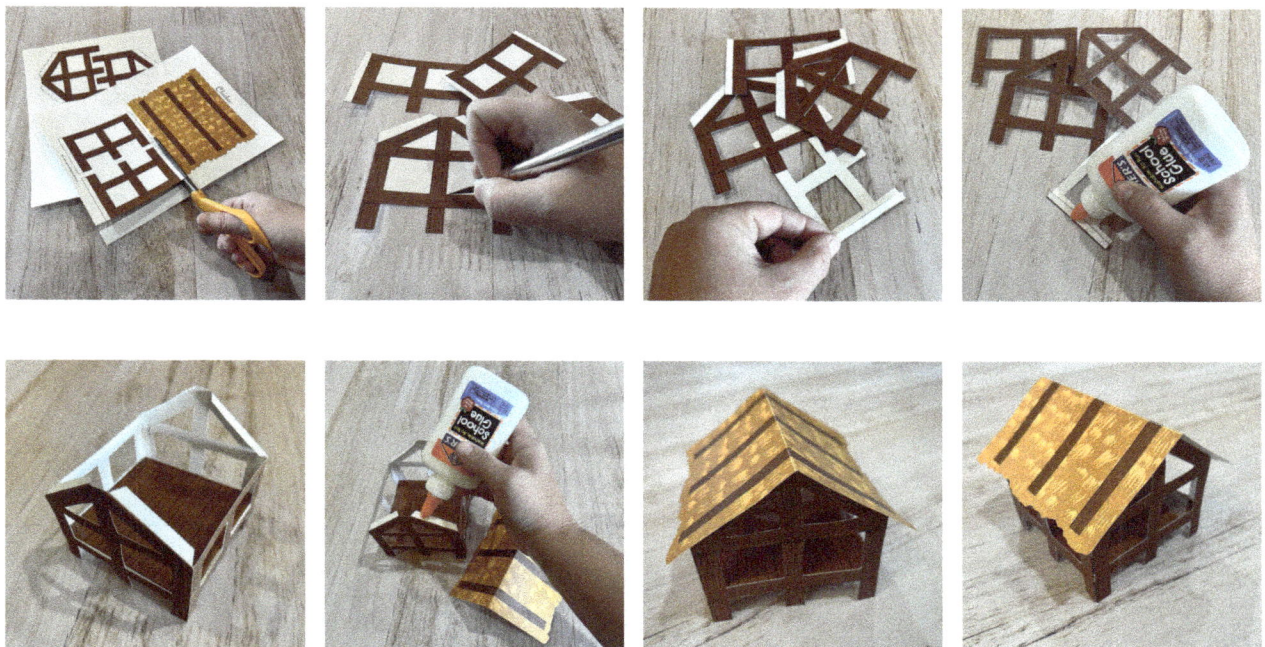

Chickee

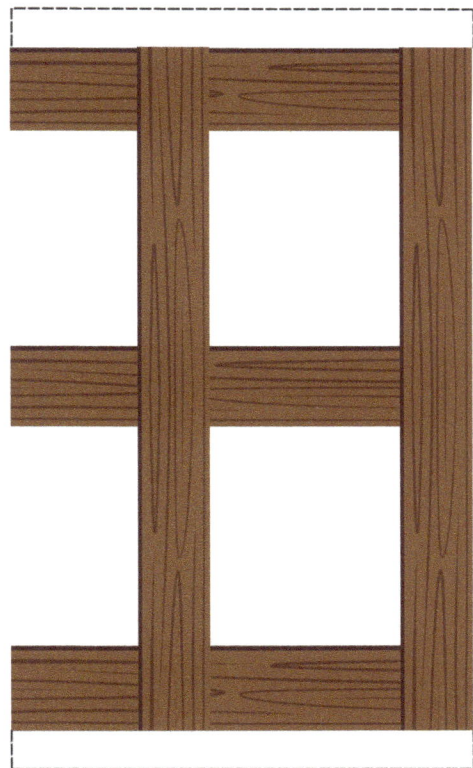

Chickee

IGLOO MODEL

Instructions

The Igloo is a type of dome-shaped shelter built from blocks of solid snow, traditionally used by Inuits, or the Native Americans of the arctic. Igloos provide good protection in the polar region, where the earth is frozen, the snow cover is deep, and there are few trees. Snow is a good insulator, and dense blocks of ice offer good protection against the arctic winds.

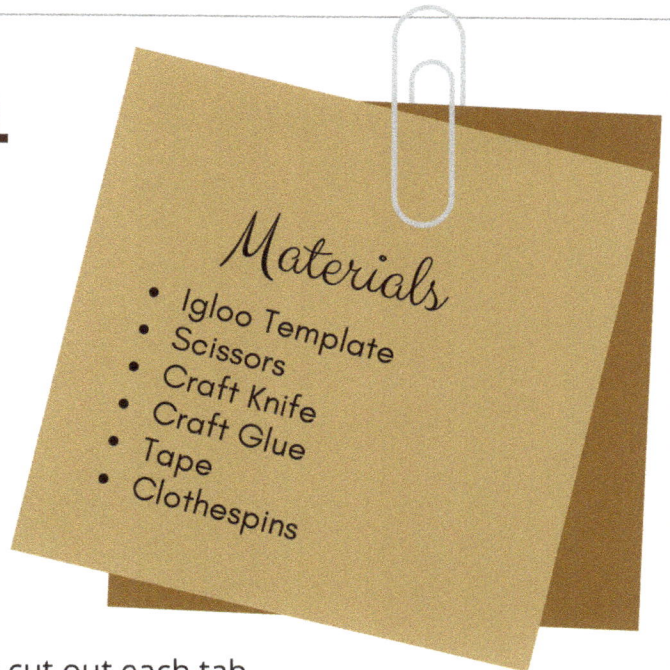

Materials

- Igloo Template
- Scissors
- Craft Knife
- Craft Glue
- Tape
- Clothespins

Cut out included igloo template. Carefully cut out each tab in between each section. Use a craft knife to cut along slits around entrance hole - *this step should be completed by an adult or with close adult supervision to avoid injury*. Fold the tabs slightly so they can accommodate the curvature of the structure. Starting at the center, glue each tab under the adjacent section to form a domed surface. Secure with craft glue, or for faster construction use tape. If using craft glue, hold pieces in place with clothespins as they dry. Fold the front entrance tunnel and secure on bottom with tab. Insert tabs of entrance into slits cut along side of entrance hole. Secure in place with glue or tape.

Igloo

PLANKHOUSE MODEL

Instructions

Plankhouses are Native American homes used by tribes of the Northwest coast. Plank houses are made of long, flat planks of cedar wood lashed to a wooden frame. Although Native American plank houses resemble old European houses, this style of house was used on the Northwest Coast long before Europeans arrived.

Cut out included plankhouse template pieces. Fold the tabs along the side and front and back pieces. Attach together with glue or tape along sides to create a four-sided structure. It may be helpful to use clothespins to secure pieces during drying process. Allow structure to completely dry before proceeding to next step. Fold roof piece in half, as indicated. Secure to base alone tabs, and allow to dry completely. **Discuss:** What is your house made of? What are some common materials used to make houses in your area?

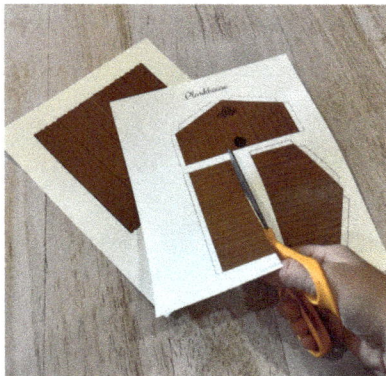

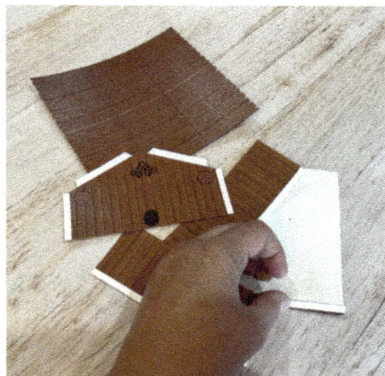

Plankhouse

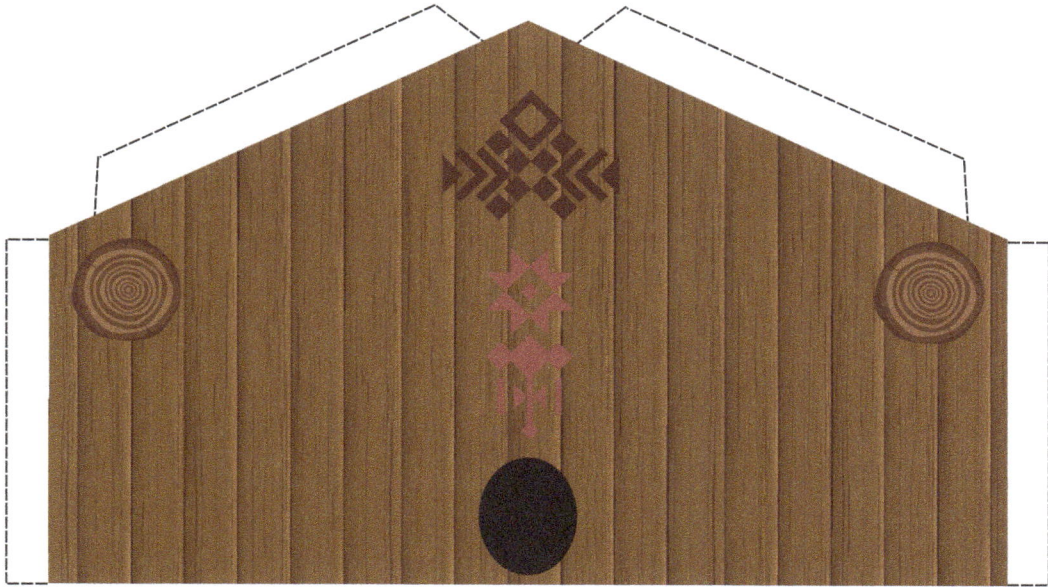

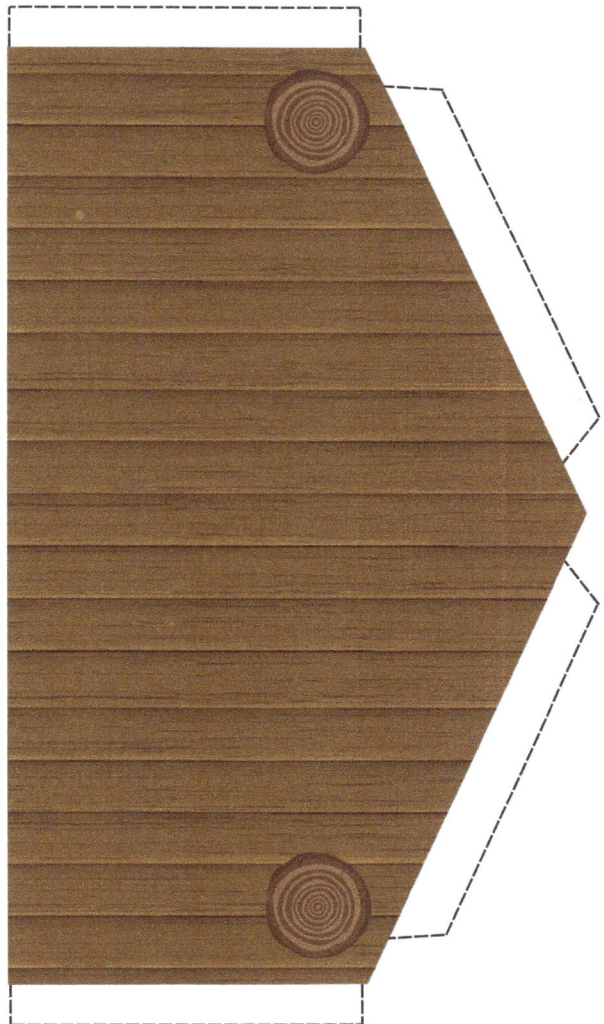

Plankhouse

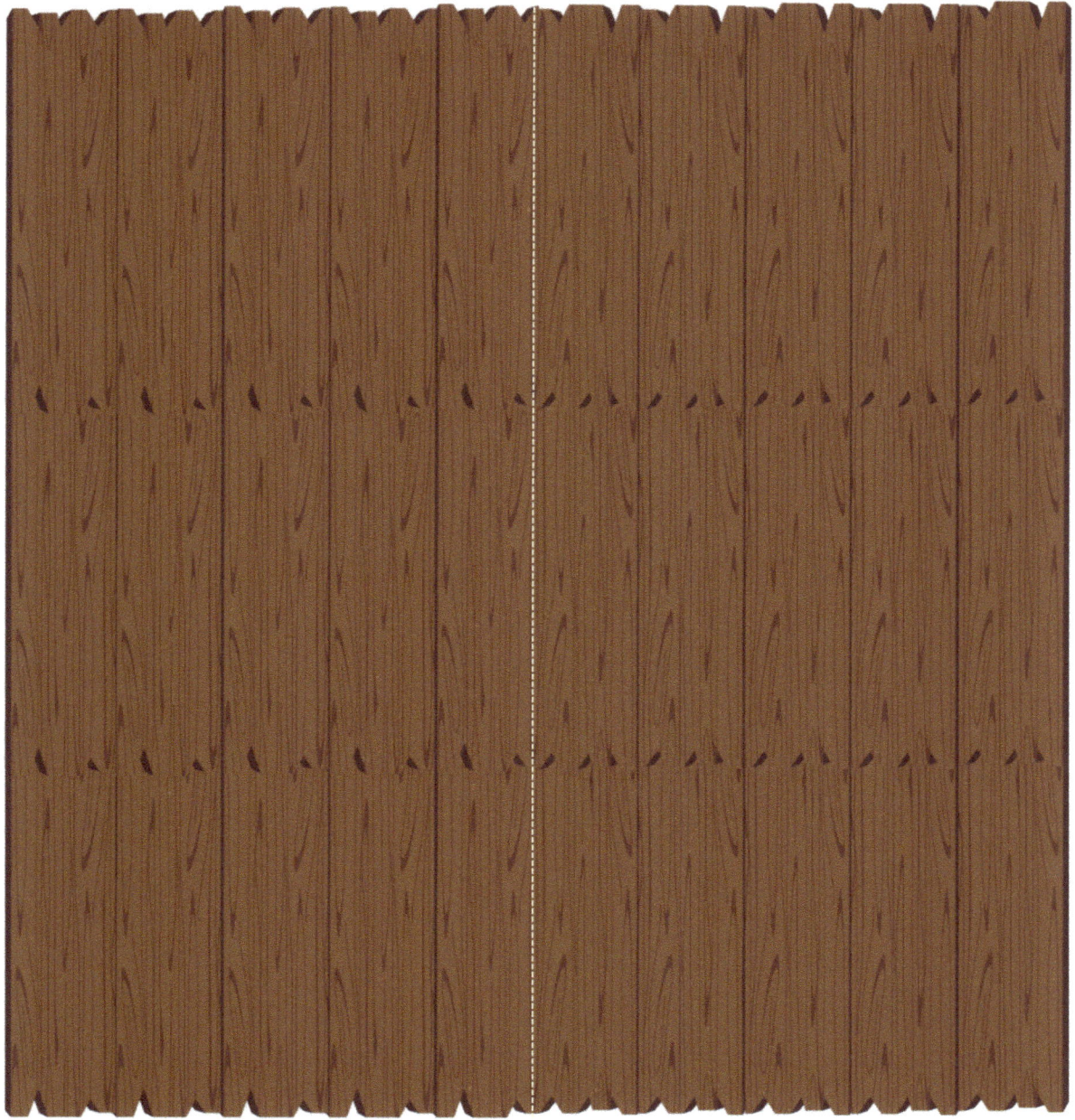

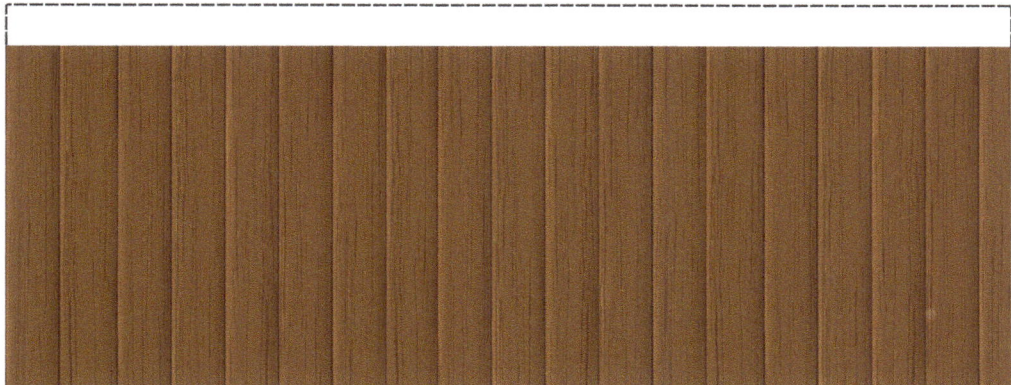

NATIVE AMERICAN SENSORY BIN

Instructions

Materials
- Sand
- Feathers
- Terracotta Pot(s)
- Sticks
- Rocks
- Beads
- Arrowheads

North America is littered with historical sites, each with tiny bits of history waiting to be told. This sensory bin mimics an archeological find, a way to learn about the past and the first people of North America.

Start with a layer of sand - you can use almost any kind of sand. Next add small sticks, rocks, feathers, and colored beads. Take a couple small terracotta pots and draw or paint a few drawings. Smash into medium size chunks and sand any rough edges so that little fingers are safe. Add arrowheads for a final touch.

Pretend to be archeologists - use your imagination! What can we learn from studying this place? Can the pot be put back together? Examine the arrowheads.

North America Fauna (3-Part Cards)

Black Bear

Bald Eagle

Appolosa Horse

Turtle

North America Fauna (3-Part Cards)

Black Bear

Bald Eagle

Appolosa Horse

Turtle

North America Fauna (3-Part Cards)

Bison

Beaver

Wolf

Golden Eagle

North America Fauna (3-Part Cards)

Bison

Beaver

Wolf

Golden Eagle

NORTH AMERICAN ANIMAL TRACKS

Instructions

Tracking was an important skill for many Native Americans. This ability helped them successfully locate and hunt food as well as avoid detection and learn information from other tribes and later settlers.

6 Cups Flour
1 Cup Cocoa Powder
1/2 Cup Coffee Grounds
1 Cups Oil

Combine above ingredients to form a crumbly dirt-like mixture. Place in shallow pan or casserole dish. Arrange the track cards nearby and have the child try to recreate the animal print in the "dirt" - excellent for early writing skill development and replication abilities. Ask the child if they have seen the animal and what they know about them. Have another child or adult create a track and have the other child try to guess which track it is.

North American Animal Tracks

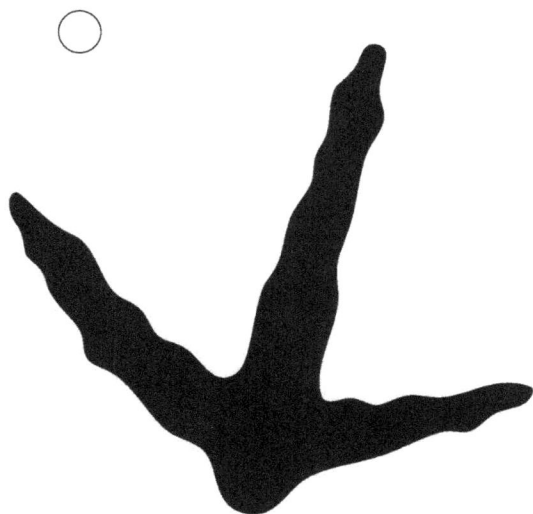

turkey

tortoise

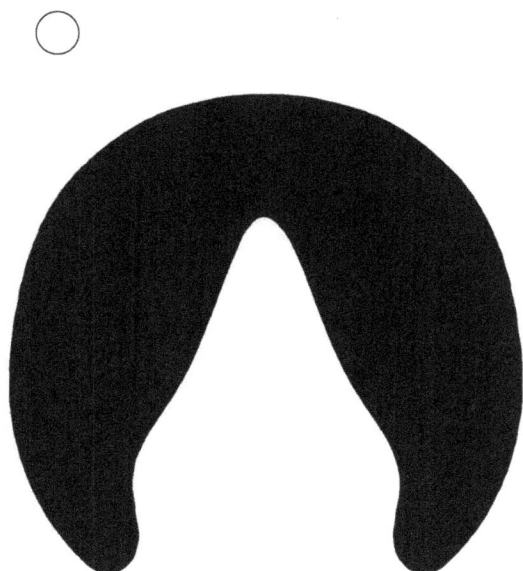

horse

hare

North American Animal Tracks

eagle

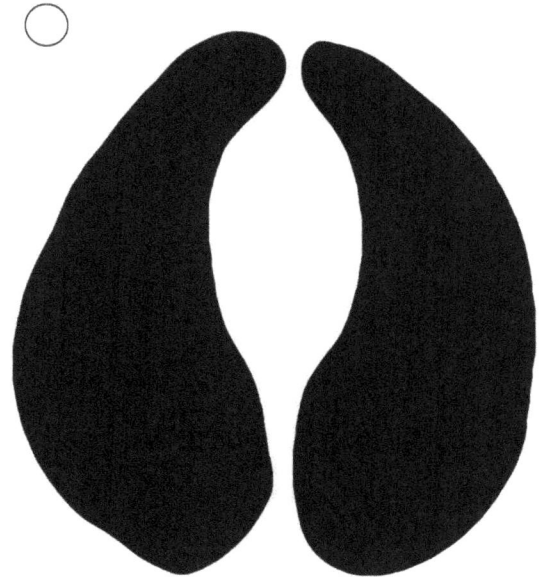

bison

bear

beaver

North American Animal Tracks

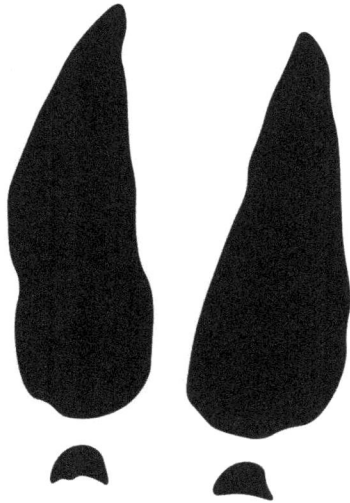

deer

raccoon

wolf

fox

Life Cycle Spinner

Life Cycle of the Bison

rump

back

hump

horns

eyes

nose

adolescent

calf

adult

pregnant

mouth

hooves

legs

mane

Parts of the Bison

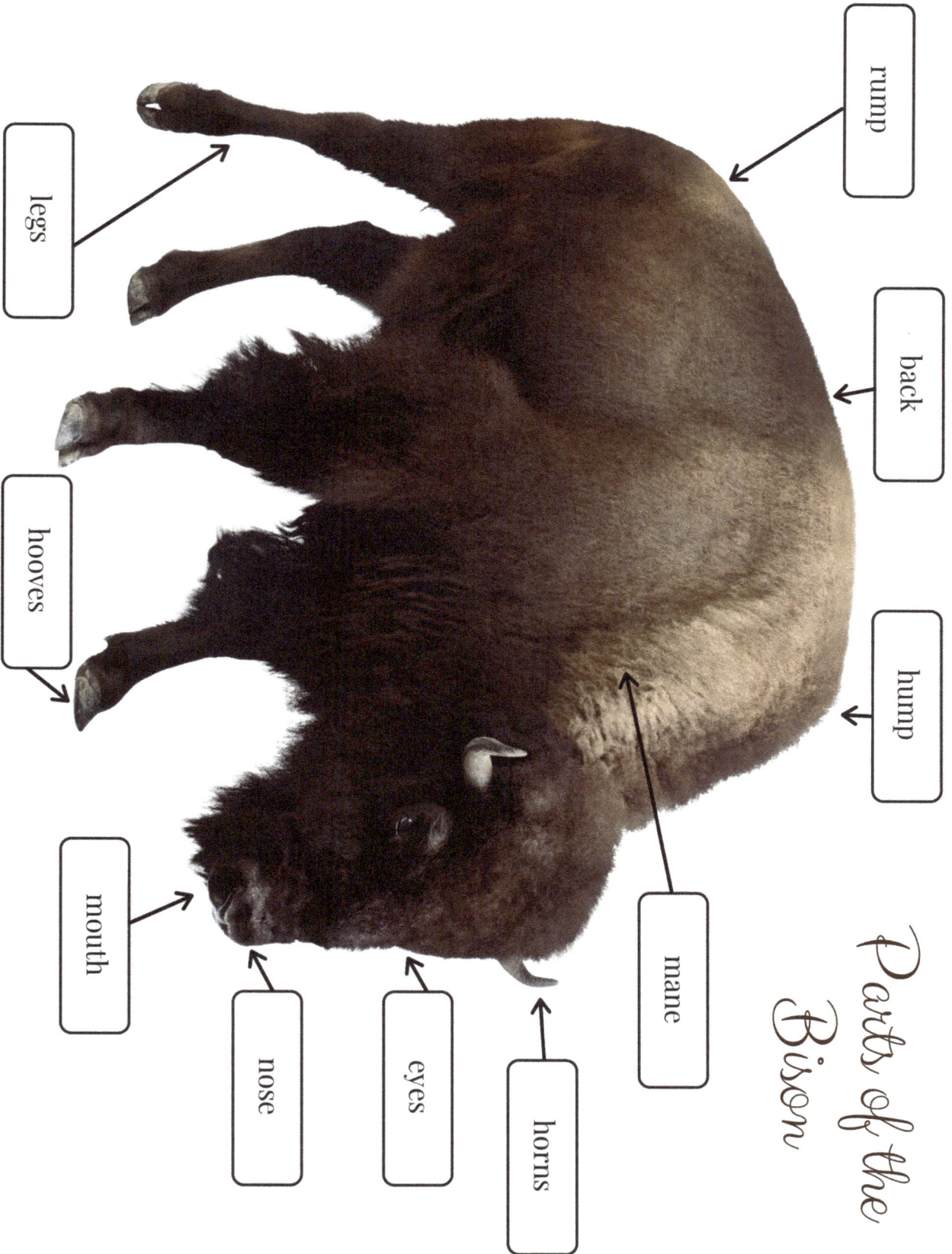

rump

back

hump

mane

horns

eyes

nose

mouth

hooves

legs

Parts of the Bison

Learning to Write

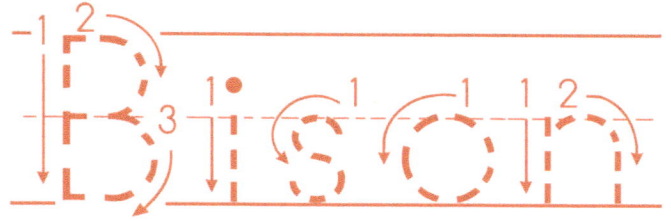

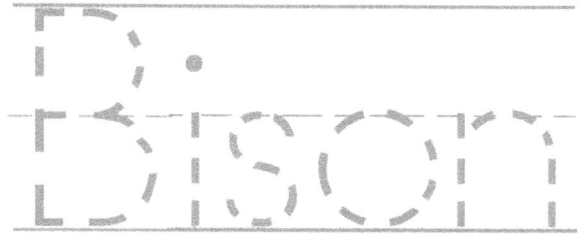

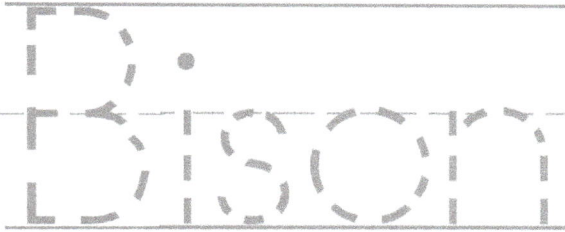

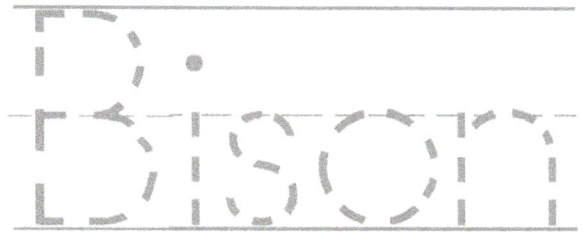

Bison

Bison

Bison

Bison

Bison

Bison

Bison

Bison versus Buffalo

Bison

- Horns: Small & Sharp
- Shoulders: Hump
- Heads: Bigger
- Chin: Beard
- Coat: Thick and Wooly (sheds in summer)
- Tail: Shorter
- Habitat: North America & Europe
- Weight: Up to 2,200 pounds
- Height: Up to 6 feet
- Lifespan: 13 to 21 years

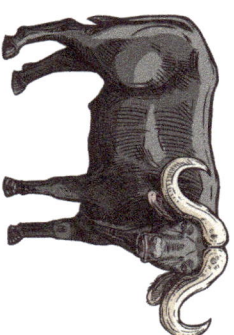

(Shared)

- Large, ox-like creatures
- *Bovidae* family
- Cloven-hoofed
- Diet: Grass
- Gestation Period: About 10-11 months
- Males called bulls, females called cows

Buffalo

- Horns: Long & Curved
- Shoulders: No Hump
- Heads: Smaller
- Chin: No Beard
- Coat: Thin and smooth - does not shed
- Tail: Longer
- Habitat: Asia and Africa
- Weight: Up to 2,000 pounds
- Height: Up to 5 feet
- Lifespan: 15 to 30 years

Buffalo Mask

Cut out mask. Cut out indicated eyeholes. Glue onto craft stick and use as a mask. Pretend to be the animal – what sounds do they make? How do they move?

BISON FELT PUZZLE

Instructions

The American bison is the most significant animal to many American Indian nations. For thousands of years, Native Americans relied heavily on bison for their survival and well-being, using every part of the bison for food, clothing, shelter, tools, jewelry and in ceremonies.

Cut out included bison patterns. Lay patterns onto indicated felt pieces and trace around the pattern. Cut out each piece; be careful to cute with detail so the pattern pieces fit together appropriately. Place the base piece down first. Add the head, mane and tail next. Then put on the horn, eye circle and eye, nose and hooves. For younger children it may be appropriate to glue the small eye, nose and hoof pieces to avoid them becoming lost.

Provide the child with included anatomy tags. Have them correctly identify the different features of the bison.

Materials
- Bison Pattern
- Scissors
- Grey, Tan, Brown, Chocolate & Black Felt
- Marker

Bison Puzzle Pattern

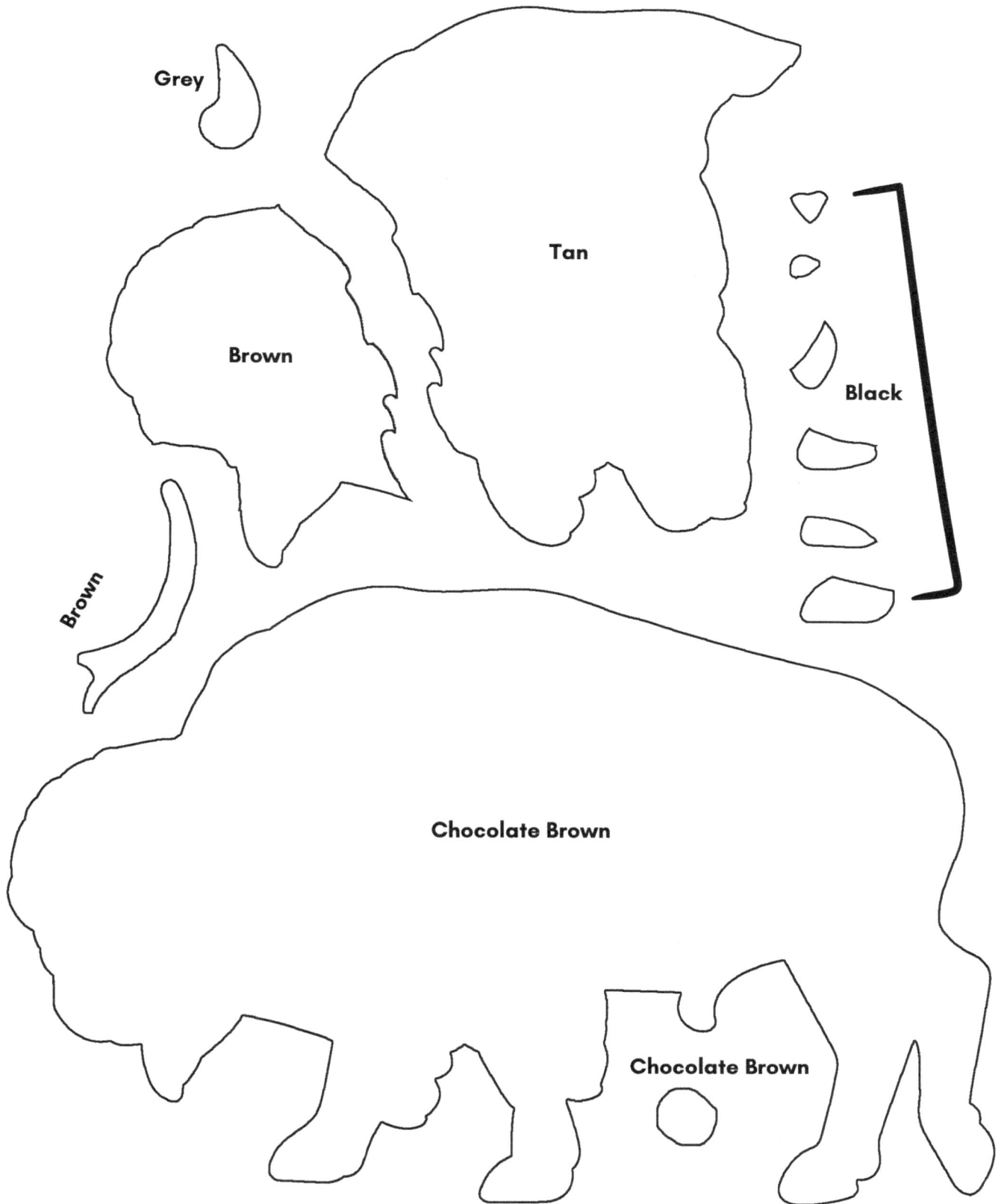

Grey

Tan

Brown

Black

Brown

Chocolate Brown

Chocolate Brown

BOW & ARROW CRAFT

Instructions

The bow and arrow is a weapon consisting of a flexible launching device and long-shafted projectile. Native American's used bow and arrows because they allowed rapid missile velocity, high degree of accuracy, and could be created with minimal supplies. Even as the gun was introduced into their culture, the arrows are much quieter than guns, allowing the hunter more chances to strike at the prey.

Using a 2-3 foot green stick, found in nature, notch holes on top and bottom and thread string to form a taunt base, slightly bending the stick. It's important to use a green stick as a full dry one will break. Decorate the "bow" with feathers and beads as desired. To create the arrows, use 1 foot sticks, making sure they are as straight as possible. Notch one end and secure an arrowhead to the end. If needed, cut arrowheads out of stiff paper or cardboard. Create a small notch at the opposite end to allow the arrow to sit on the bow string securely. See photos for more detail.

With adult supervision and safe open area, attempt to launch arrows.

Discuss: Consider the thrust provided by the bow string, how does pulling this back affect the flight of the arrow? How accurate does the arrow fly?

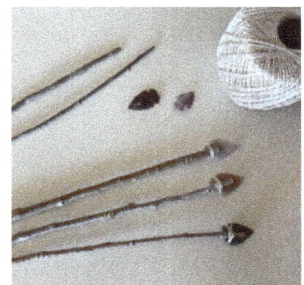

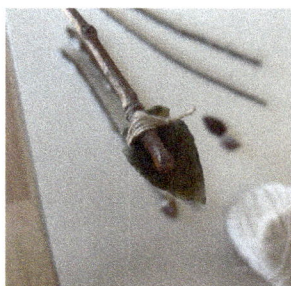

Materials
- Green Tree Stick
- 4-6 Straight Sticks
- Knife
- Beads
- Feathers
- Arrowheads
- String

Finish the Pattern: Arrowheads

Finish the Pattern: Arrowheads

POTATO ARROWHEAD CARVING

Instructions

Arrowheads have been used by Native Americans for centuries, as both a weapon and a tool. Native Americans chose stones that could be easily chipped and sharpened. Most arrowheads were made from various stones such as flint and obsidian.

Provide child with a small/medium sized, washed potato. For younger children, peel the potato first; older children can peel their own. Provide the child with a child-safe knife to carve the potato. It is recommended that adults supervise this step because even with child-safe knives, injuries can occur. Have the child carve away from their hands into a pointed tip. Continue to remove from the top and bottom until an arrowhead shape forms. Cut notches in the back where the arrowhead would be attached to a pole or stick. Compare with arrowhead designs.
Suggestion: Wash potato remnants and use in a potato dish to eat.

The Three Sisters

The Three Sisters (corn, beans, and squash) have been planted together by traditional Native American gardeners. The corn provides a structure for the beans to climb. The beans provide nitrogen for the soil, and the squash spreads along the ground preventing weeds. This is a form of companion planting.

CORN KERNAL REMOVAL

Instructions

This activity is very simple, but provides excellent fine motor development and learning persistence. Consider doing this activity on the floor to minimize kernels flying too far from overzealous little fingers.

Have the child use tweezers to pull off only one kernel at a time. For younger children, try to take off one kernel at a time with their fingers. Try to remove an entire row at a time. Count the kernels; how many has the child removed? How many still needs to be removed?

Note: Feed corn is the most economical way to prepare for this activity. The discarded husks can be used for other activities and the corn can be fed to wildlife.

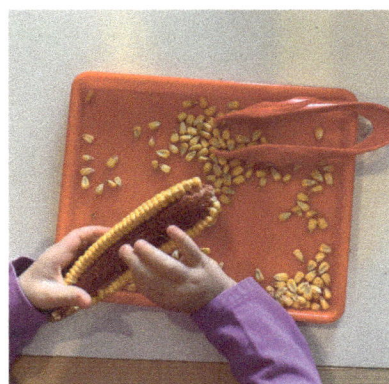

Materials

- Dried Corncobs
- Tweezers
- Tray

BEADED RAINBOW CORN

Instructions

Flint corn, sometimes referred to as Indian or rainbow corn, is one of the oldest varieties of corn, a type that Native Americans taught the early colonists how to cultivate. The kernels come in a range of colors including white, blue and red, and have a hard "flint like" shell, giving this corn its name.

Materials

- Pipe-cleaners
- Pony Beads, Assorted

Take 3-4 pipe-cleaners. Green, brown or tan pipe-cleaners are recommended as they most closely resemble corn husks. Provide child(ren) with colorful pony beads - almost any color will work for this activity. It may be helpful to show the child photos of flint corn for inspiration. Have child thread random assortment of beads until 1.5-2" of of pipe-cleaner remains. Repeat on other strands. Fold the beaded strands so they are even and twist the tops together. Adjust to appear like corn silk coming off the top. Make multiple "ears" using different colors.

CORN HUSK DOLL

Instructions

A corn husk doll is a Native American doll made out of the dried leaves or "husk" of a corn cob. Brittle dried cornhusks become soft if soaked in water and produce finished dolls sturdy enough for children's toys, and can be twisted together to form a doll-shaped toy. Corn silk can be used for hair.

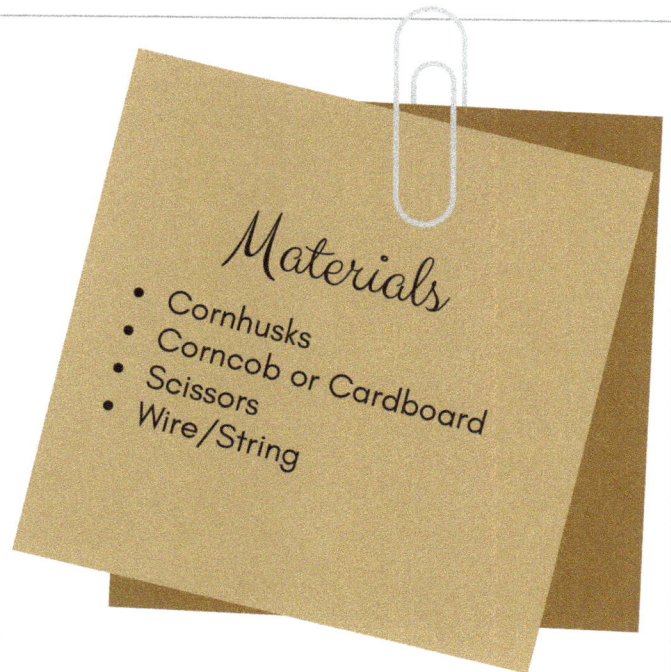

Using a corncob or piece of cardboard as a base, fold over a piece of cornhusk to form the head. Secure in place with a length of cornhusk or a small piece of wire or string as pictured. Twist a small length of cornhusk to form the "arms" - thread this under the "neck" and secure with another length of string or wire. Crisscross a piece of cornhusk to cover up wire/string and appear like a top of dress. Trim bottom of doll to create the appearance of a dress. **Discuss:** How does a cornhusk doll compare to modern dolls?

PAPER ROLL TOTEM

Instructions

A totem is a spirit being, sacred object, or symbol that serves as an emblem of a group of people, such as a family, clan, lineage, or tribe. Native Americans would meticulously carve intricate faces into wood that paid homage to ancestors and events. Due to the time and effort needed to create these, they were often found near wealthier homes, such as chiefs.

Materials

- Totem Cutouts
- Markers, Crayons or Paints
- Scissors
- Cardboard Tube
- Glue
- Tape

Provide child with totem cutouts and allow them to color with markers, crayons or paints. Cut out each totem piece. Fold the tabs on each side of the wings and glue onto indicated space, as pictured. Wrap around cardboard tube, allowing enough space to slide easily. Secure with tape and repeat with other sections. Have child slide totem pieces over cardboard tube. How does the totem look if the pieces are "mixed up?" What does the child think the images portray?

Totem Template

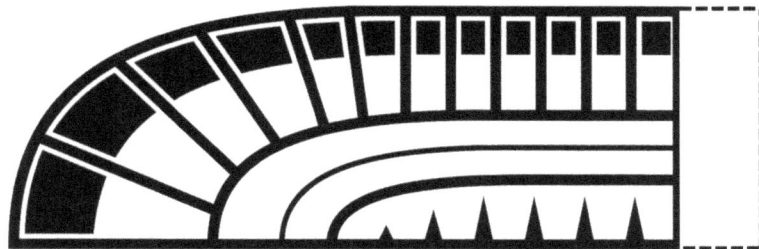

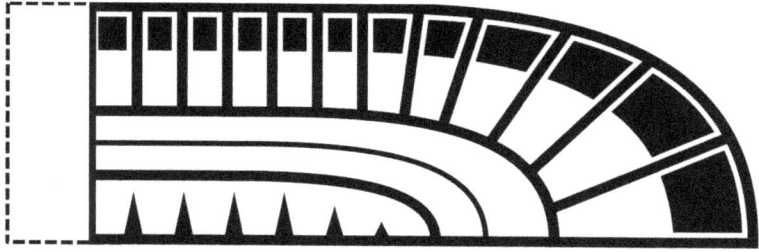

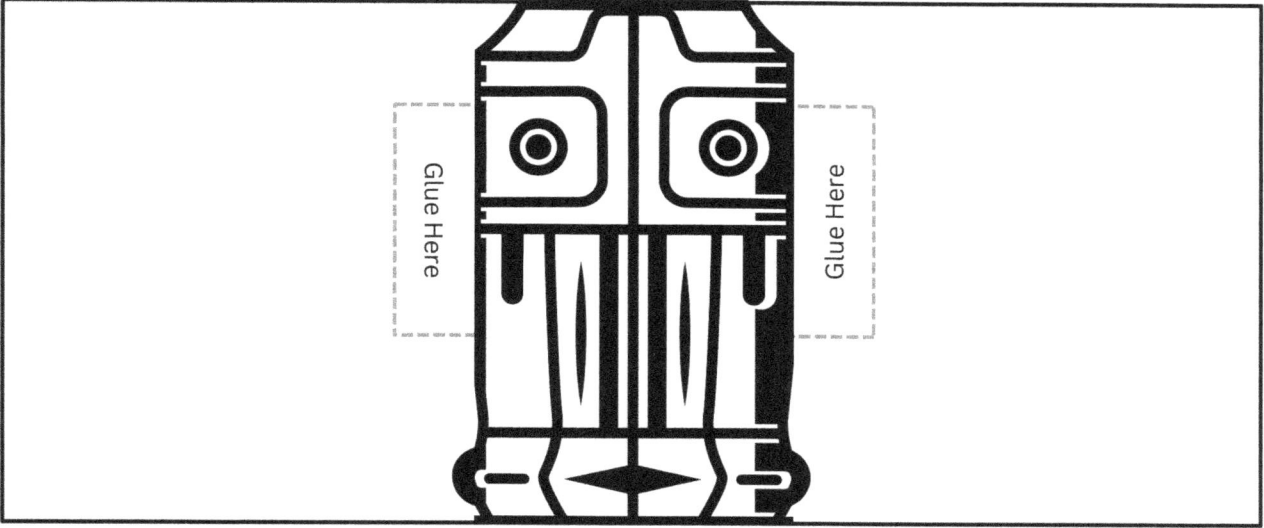

Glue Here

Glue Here

GOURD DRUMS

Instructions

Drums are an important part of music and ceremonies in the Native American culture. Traditionally these drums were created from hollowed-out logs, with hides stretched taut across the opening secured by additional leather.

Cut the ends off several decorative gourds. Have the child scoop the insides out and allow them to dry for a week or so.

Materials
- Gourds
- Knife/Spoon
- Craft Paper/Cloth
- Hole Punch
- String
- Sticks
- Clay
- Cloth

Trace the open side of the gourd onto paper or cloth. Cut out slightly wider than tracing to allow for overlap around gourd. If using paper, use a hole punch to create holes to secure to gourd. Create a second piece for opposite end or just wrap around base as its laced into place. If using cloth, use a needle and thick thread to secure. For younger children, provide assistance. For other children this process is great fine motor work. Secure covering in place. Create drum sticks from sticks or sticks covered with a bit of clay covered in cloth for muted sound. **Discuss:** How do the different drums sound - how does the sound vary?

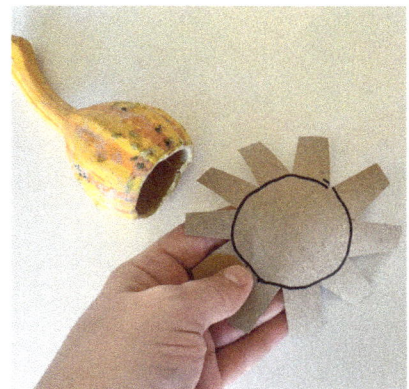

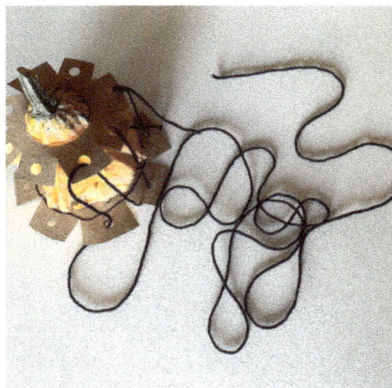

DREAM CATCHER

Instructions

In many Native American tribes, a dream catcher is a handmade willow hoop woven to a web or literally, a net, and decorated with feathers and beads. Dream catchers can be traced back to the Ojibwes, which crafted them for protection or to "catch" bad spirits and dreams, especially for young children, and were often positioned over their beds.

Materials

- Dream Catcher Template
- Markers / Crayons
- Laminator (optional)
- Hole Punch
- String/Yarn

Color included dream catcher template. Laminate if desired for additional durability. Cut out all included pieces. Punch holes in indicated places. Attach three feathers to the bottom of the dream catcher with string. Lace inside of dream catcher to form a web. Younger children may need additional assistance. Thread a small hanger through hole on top of circle. Hang completed dream catcher from ceiling with a thumb-tack or adhere to wall.

Dream Catcher

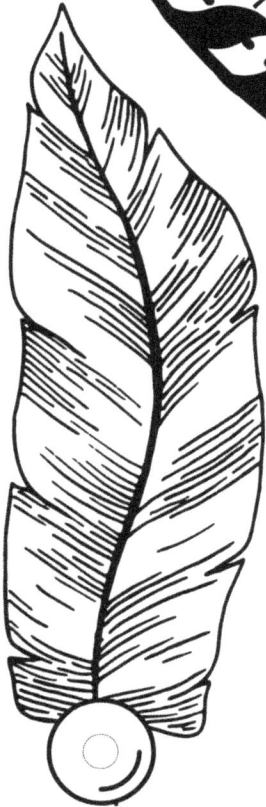

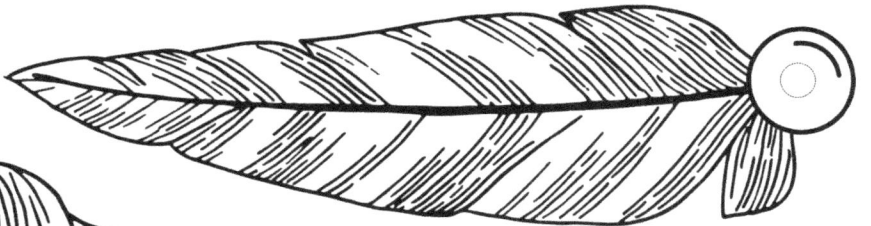

Native American Warrior

Headaddress

Hair Tie

Breastplate
Beads

War Shirt

Gloves

Arrow

Bow

Leggings

Moccasins

Moccasin Lacing

Cut out included moccasin, punch holes where indicated and have have child "sew" around exterior with a shoelace or piece of yarn.

FRY BREAD

ingredients

- 3 Cups Vegetable Oil
- 1 Cup Flour (*plus additional*)
- 1.5 Teaspoons Baking Powder
- 1/4 Teaspoon Salt
- 1/2 Cup Milk

directions

- Heat oil in frying pan until hot.
- Combine the flour, baking powder, and salt in a bowl. Blend well.
- Add milk and stir until dough forms.
- Knead several times on a floured surface.
- Divide into four pieces and shape into balls.
- Using a lightly floured rolling pin, flatten each ball of dough to 1/4 to 1/2 inch thick.
- Carefully slide 1 or 2 pieces of dough into the hot oil. Fry for about 1 to 2 minutes on each side, or until lightly browned.
- ***NOTE: oil can cause BURNS and this step should be completed by an adult!**
- Remove the fried dough to paper towels to drain.
- Serve with vegetables or sprinkled with cinnamon and sugar as a desert.

Adult Supervision Required

Fry Bread

INGREDIENTS

3 CUPS VEGETABLE OIL

1 CUP FLOUR (PLUS ADDITIONAL)

1.5 TEASPOONS BAKING POWDER

1/4 TEASPOON SALT

1/2 CUP MILK

Historic Native Americans

Tisquantum

Pocahontas

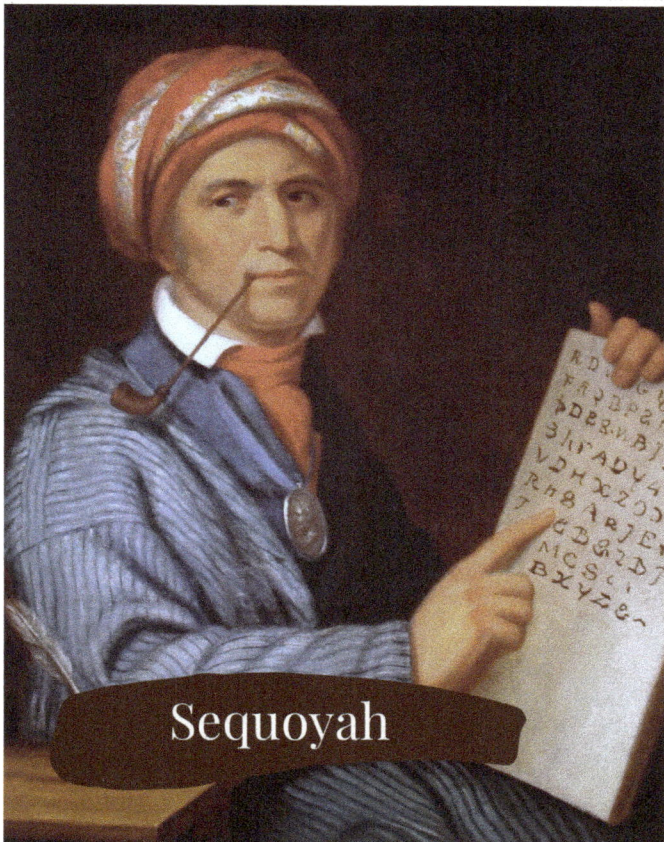

Sequoyah

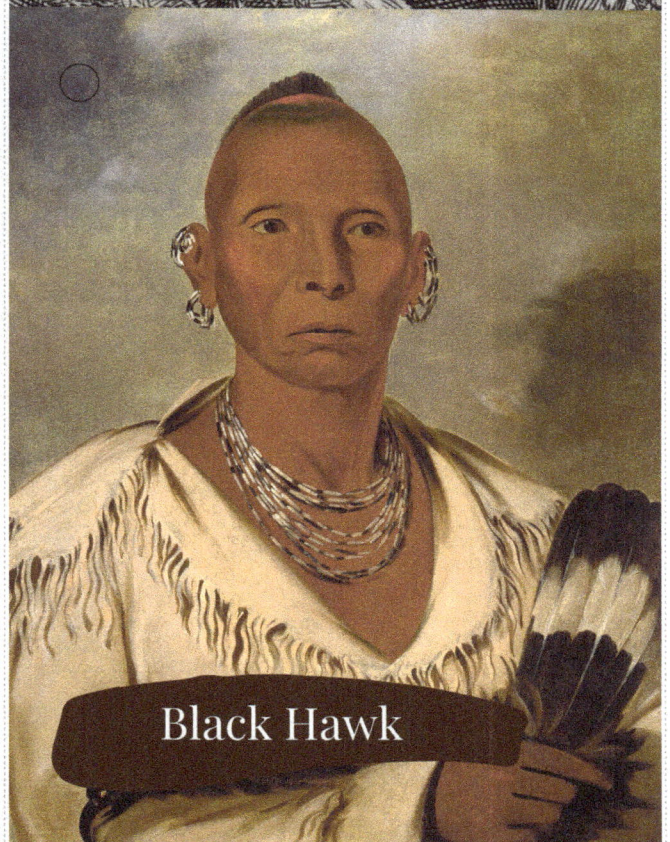

Black Hawk

Pocahontas

Born: 1595
Died: March 1617
Tribe: Powhatan

Pocahontas was a Native American woman of the Powhatan People. She is known for her association with the colonial settlement at Jamestown, Virginia. Pocahontas was captured and held for ransom by the Colonists during hostilities in 1613. During her captivity, she was baptized under the name Rebecca. She was married to tobacco planter John Rolfe, and had a son Thomas Rolfe. She and her husband traveled to London where Pocahontas was presented to English society as an example of a "civilized" Indian in hopes of stimulating investment in the Jamestown settlement.

Tisquantum (Squanto)

Born: 1585
Died: November 30, 1622
Tribe: Patuxet

Tisquantum, commonly known by Squanto, is best known for helping the Mayflower Pilgrims. Tisquantum was initially kidnapped and sold as a slave in Spain. He was among a number of captives bought by local monks who focused on their education and evangelization. When he finally returned to his native village in 1619, he learned his tribe had been wiped out by an epidemic infection; Around a year later, the Pilgrims arrived and settled in Plymouth near Squanto's tribe. Since Squanto could speak English he helped establish a treaty between the local Native Americans and the Pilgrims, and taught them valuable survival skills.

Black Hawk

Born: 1767
Died: October 3, 1838
Tribe: Sauk

Black Hawk was a capable and fierce war Chief. During the War of 1812, Black Hawk fought on the side of the British against the US in the hope of pushing white American settlers away from Sauk territory. Later, he led a band of Sauk and Fox warriors, known as the British Band, against white settlers in Illinois and present-day Wisconsin during the 1832 Black Hawk War. After the war, he was captured by US forces. Shortly before being released from custody, Black Hawk told his story to an interpreter, and published his autobiography, which became a bestseller.

Sequoyah

Born: 1775
Died: August 1843
Tribe: Cherokee

Sequoyah is known for his independent creation of the Cherokee syllabary, making reading and writing in Cherokee possible. He is one of few that have created original, effective writing system from a pre-literate language. His creation of the Syllabary allowed the Cherokee nation to be one of the first North American Indigenous groups to have a written language. Sequoyah was also an important representative for the Cherokee nation, by going to Washington, D.C. to sign two relocations and trading of land treaties.

Historic Native Americans

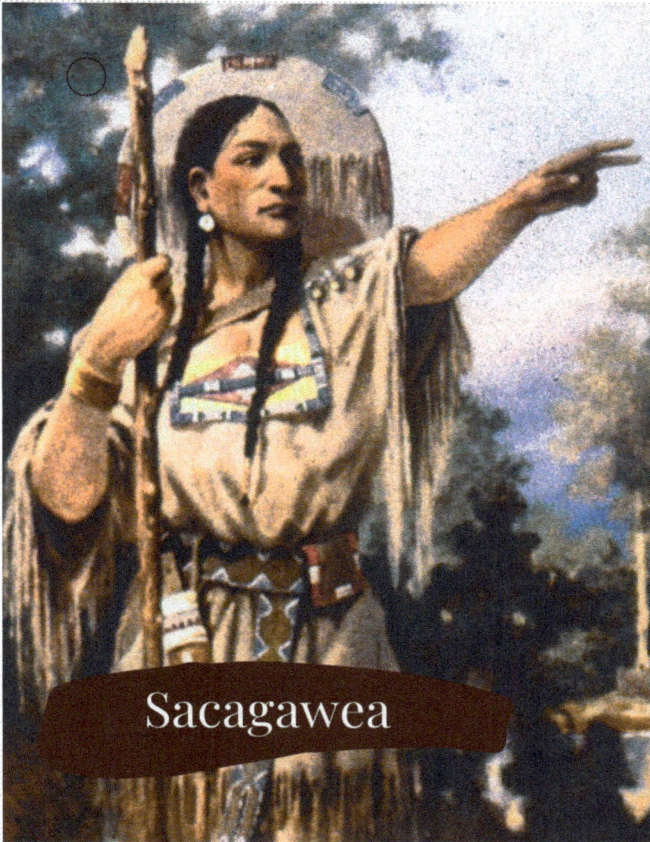
Sacagawea

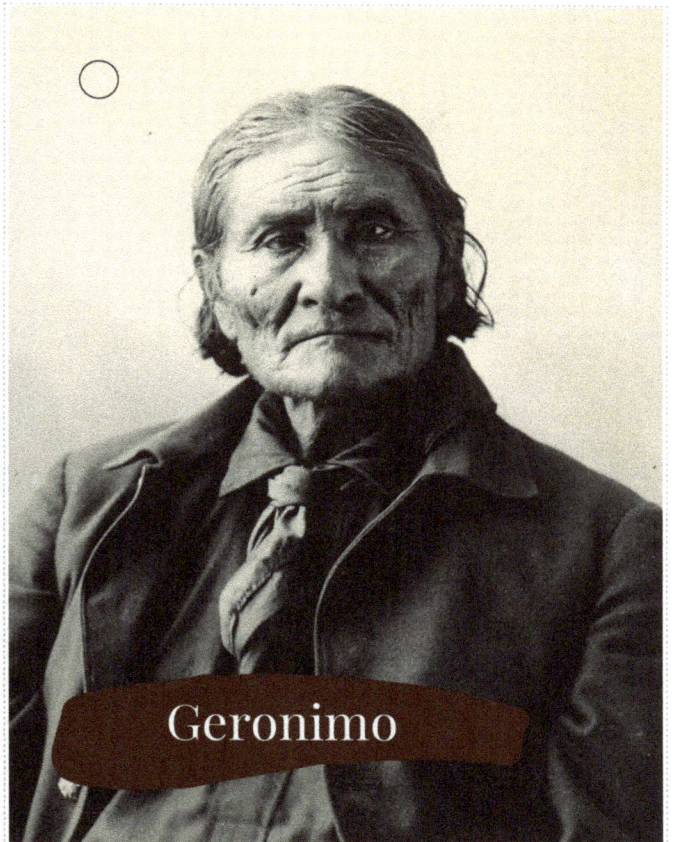
Geronimo

Sitting Bull

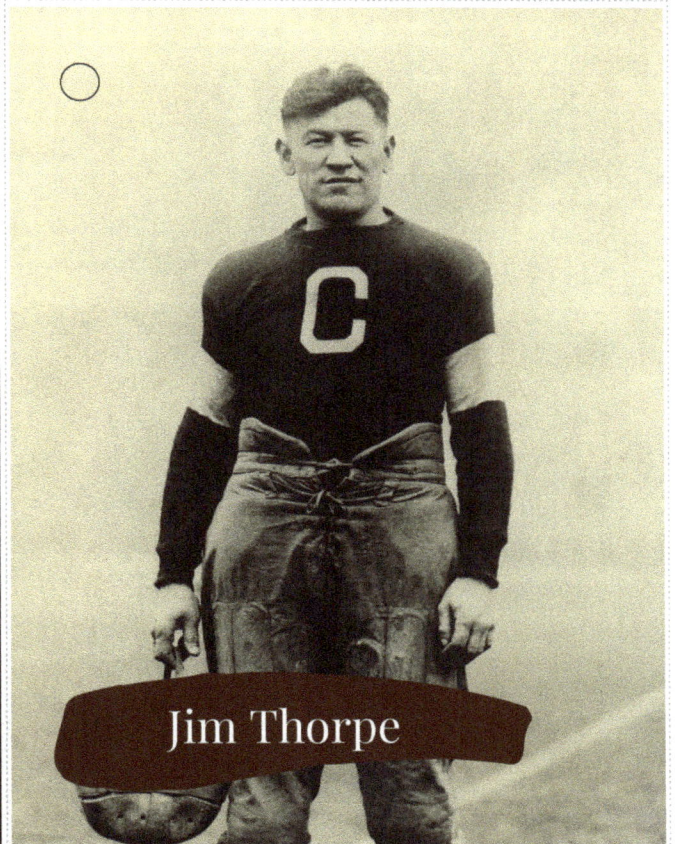
Jim Thorpe

Geronimo

Born: June 16, 1829
Died: February 17, 1909
Tribe: Apache

Geronimo was a prominent leader and medicine man. His name means "one who yawns". Although he was not a chief, he was a superb leader in raiding and warfare, and frequently led large numbers of men beyond his own following. Geronimo led the Apache in stiff resistance for many years against both invaders from the west and from Mexico. He was eventually captured and lived the remainder of his life as a prisoner of war to the United States Army.

Sacagawea

Born: May 1788
Died: December 20, 1812
Tribe: Shoshone

Sacagawea assisted the Lewis and Clark Expedition in achieving their chartered mission objectives by exploring the Louisiana Territory. Sacagawea helped introduce Native American populations to settlers and helped the expedition's knowledge of natural history. In the early 1900s, The National American Woman Suffrage Association used her as a symbol of women's worth and independence, erecting several statues and plaques in her memory, and doing much to recount her accomplishments.

Jim Thorpe

Born: May 22, 1887
Died: March 28, 1953
Tribe: Sac and Fox Nation

Jim Thorpe grew up in Oklahoma, and is considered one of the greatest athletes of all time. He played professional baseball, basketball, and football. He also won Olympic Gold Medals for the pentathlon and decathlon in the 1912 Olympics. Thorpe appeared in several films and was portrayed in the 1951 film *Jim Thorpe - All-American.*

Sitting Bull

Born: 1831
Died: December 15, 1890
Tribe: Sioux

Sitting Bull was a leader of the Lakota Sioux Plains Indians who led his people during years of resistance against United States government policies. He had a vision that the Sioux would win a great battle against the white man. He led a combined group of warriors from the Lakota, Cheyenne, and Arapahoe tribes into battle. This famous battle was called the Battle of Little Big Horn and was fought against General Custer. In this battle, sometimes called Custer's Last Stand, Sitting Bull completely destroyed Custer's army.

Historic Native Americans

Will Rogers

Crazy Horse

Maria Tallchief

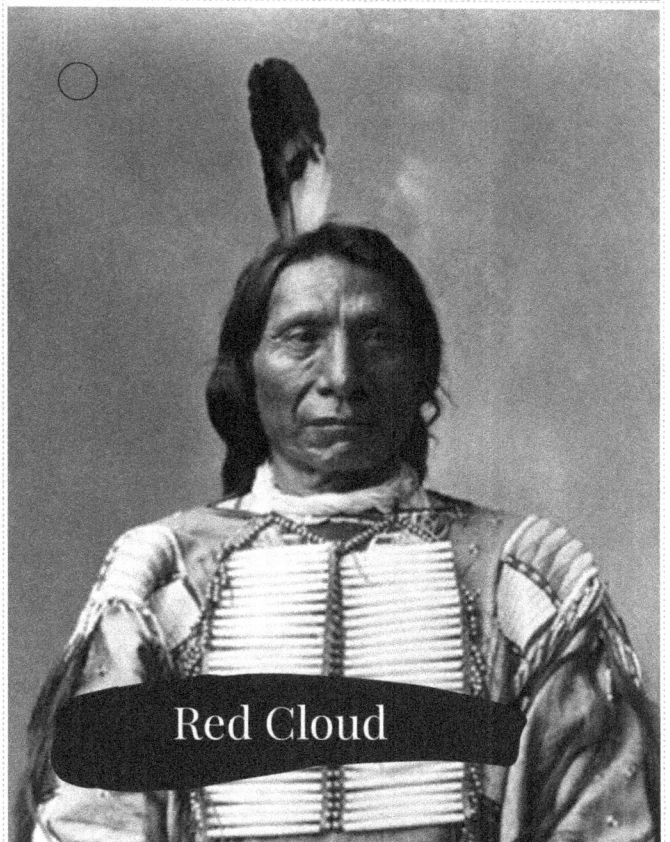

Red Cloud

Crazy Horse

Born: 1840
Died: September 5, 1877
Tribe: Lakota

Crazy Horse was a war leader who fought against the United States government to preserve the territories and traditional way of life of the Lakota people. He fought in several famous battles of the Black Hills War on the northern Great Plains, including the Fetterman Fight of 1866, in which he acted as a decoy and the Battle of the Little Bighorn in 1876, where he led a war party to victory. He was highly respected by his people and his enemies.

Will Rogers

Born: November 4, 1879
Died: August 15, 1935
Tribe: Cherokee

Will Rogers was an actor, performer, cowboy, humorist, columnist, and social commentator from Oklahoma. Born a Cherokee citizen, he was known as "Oklahoma's Favorite Son", He traveled around the world three times, made 71 films and wrote more than 4,000 nationally syndicated newspaper columns. Will was very popular in the United States for his leading political wit, and was the highest paid of Hollywood film stars. He died in a small airplane crash in northern Alaska.

Red Cloud

Born: 1822
Died: December 10, 1909
Tribe: Oglala Lakota

Red Cloud was one of the most capable Native American opponents that the United States Army faced in its mission to occupy the western territories. He defeated the United States during Red Cloud's War, which was a fight over control of the Powder River Country in northeastern Wyoming and southern Montana. The most significant battle was the Fetterman Fight, where 81 U.S. soldiers were killed; the worst military defeat suffered by the United States Army on the Great Plains to date.

Maria Tallchief

Born: January 24, 1925
Died: April 11, 2013
Tribe: Osage

Elizabeth Marie "Betty" Tallchief was an American ballerina, said to have revolutionized ballet. She was considered America's first major prima ballerina, and the first Native American to hold the rank. She traveled the world, becoming the first American to perform in Moscow's Bolshoi Theater. She made regular appearances on American TV before she retired in 1966.

NATIVE AMERICAN CANOE

Instructions

Canoes were used as a form of transportation by Native American tribes living near bodies of water. While the method of construction varies by region, most were built in the dugout and bark styles. Modern canoes look very similar to the original Native American design.

Materials
- Canoe Template
- Scissors
- Craft Glue
- Tape
- Clothespins
- Toothpicks

Cut out included template. Fold canoe base in half. Glue both ends with craft glue and allow to dry completely. It may be helpful to use clothespins to secure while trying. Cut out the paddle. Glue toothpicks along back for additional stability. Once the base has fully dried, cut out middle portion of canoe and fold down glue tabs. Add a bit of glue to each tab and insert it in the middle of the base. Secure in place until dry.

Discuss: What are some common different types of water transportation and how do they differ? What forms of water craft have you been on?

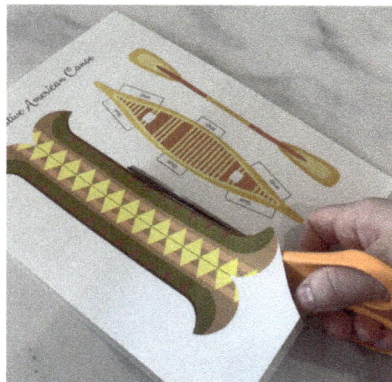

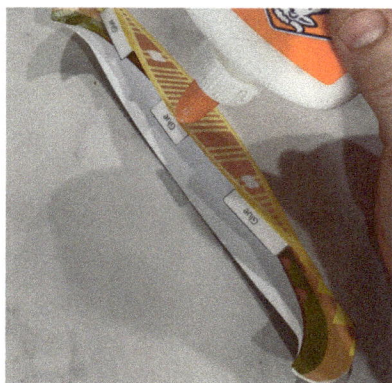

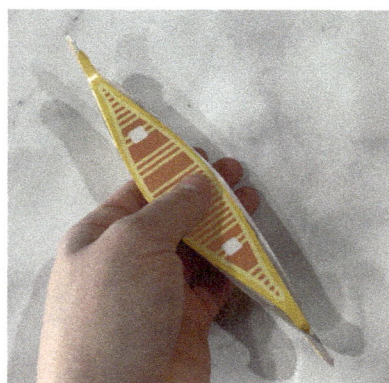

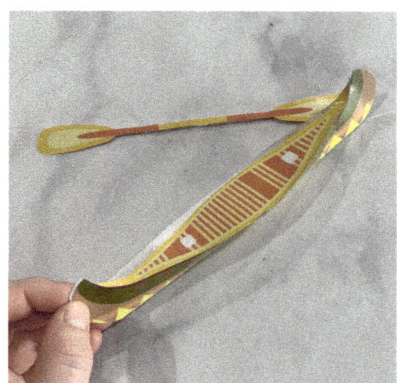

Native American Canoe

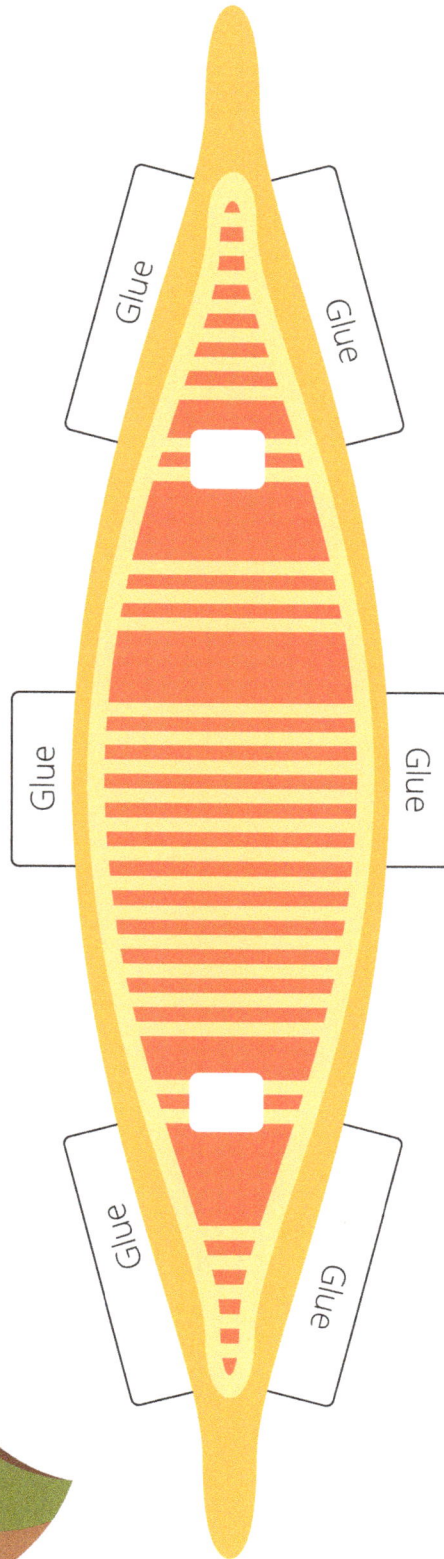

Glue

Glue

Glue

Glue

Glue

Glue

The Grasslands

Climate

Temperatures in the grasslands vary greatly, with very hot summers and very cold winters. Wind is common because the area is so flat and exposed. Fires sometimes occur , and they are often set by lightning or human activity.

Flora

Grasses dominate the grasslands, and include species such as purple needlegrass, wild oats, foxtail, ryegrass, and buffalo grass. Trees and large shrubs are found rarely. Many animals rely on these grasses for food.

Fauna

The grasslands lack shelter from predators, so fauna includes animals with hoofs and long legs to help them run fast. Animals include bison, antelope, lynx, coyotes, foxes, antelopes, birds, gophers, prairie dogs, and insects.

Water

Rain in the temperate grasslands usually occurs in the late spring and early summer. The yearly average is about 20 - 35 inches (55 - 95 cm), but much of this falls as snow in the winter.

Grasslands Habitat Match

Cut out circles of animals and match into appropriate habitat on grasslands scene.

Bald Eagle

Golden Eagle

Bison

Fox

Ferret

Wolf

Prairie Dog

Prairie Hen

Pronghorn

Burrowing Owl

Field Mouse

Hare

Badger

Rat Snake

North American Feathers

Cardinal

Horned Owl

Chickadee

Robin

Goldfinch

Bald Eagle

Golden Eagle

Canadian Goose

Turkey

Mallard Duck

Blackbird

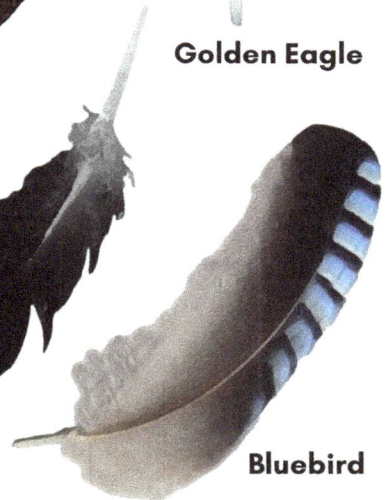

Bluebird

North American Feather Matching

Bald Eagle

Golden Eagle

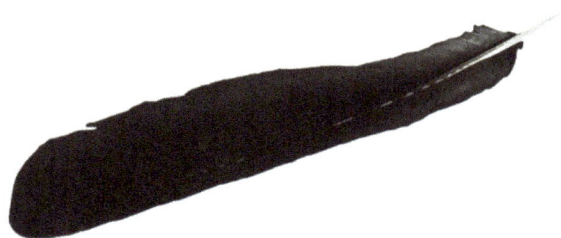

Turkey

Red Robin

North American Feather Matching

North American Feather Matching

Blackbird

Chickadee

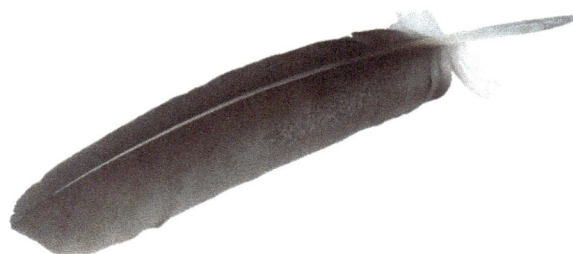

Mallard Duck

Canadian Goose

Southern Native Designs Matching

Southern Native Designs Matching

Savy
Activities

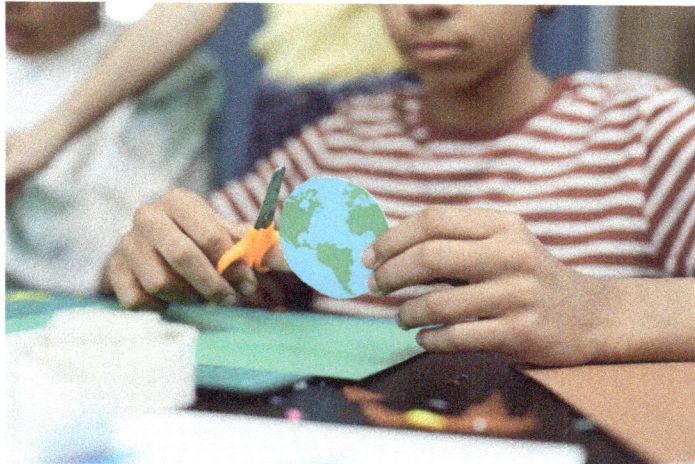

Travel the world through the interactive learning activities of **Savy Activities**; these hands-on resources provide parents, caregivers and educators practical ways to teach children about the world around them. Each book features a country, location or time period where subjects such as geography, history, vocabulary, reading, language, science, mathematics, music and art come alive by engaging auditory, visual and kinesthetic learning styles.

All activity books include geography with applicable maps, landmarks and locations. Historical events and time periods are visually represented with full color posters and flashcards, if applicable. Each book includes a set of fun-fact cards, poster and flag, if applicable. Paper models allow children to create 3D creations of major landmarks and structures. All books include a life cycle and anatomy of a plant, animal or organic compound, with flashcards and 3-part cards featuring important structures applicable to the theme.

Children learn scientific principles through active experiments and activities. Traditional customs, festivals, toys, clothing and art are also explored. Each book includes an exclusive themed mini-story featuring historical events or traditional mythology and folklore to promote vocabulary and reading. Where applicable, world languages are introduced through engaging flashcards, posters and tracing work. Each country has been meticulously researched by interviewing native persons and/or personal travel experiences to ensure the authentic culture is fully explored.

Savy Activities utilizes concepts from multiple educational methods to create unique resources allowing children a tangible and enjoyable way to explore their world. The **Savy Activities** series should not be viewed as a curriculum, but rather complimentary thematic resources to enhance traditional education. Because the individual needs and knowledge of children varies within standardized grade levels, **Savy Activities** resources have the flexibility to be used with preschool learners through early to mid-elementary years. For younger learners, adult supervision and/or assistance may be needed and activities presented in a simplified version. For older learners, resources may be paired with additional content from other materials to meet learning outcomes.

Check out our other products and resources at **www.SavyActivities.com**